A Collar In My Pocket

Blue-eyes, Brown-eyes Exercise

By Jane Elliott

ISBN: 1534619208
ISBN-13: 978-1534619203

DEDICATION

To my father, Lloyd Jennison, who made me what I am. To my husband, Darald Elliott, who married me because of what I could become. To our four children, Sarah, Brian, Mary, and Mark Elliott, who love me in spite of it all.

CONTENTS

Note: Some of what you read here is repetitious because, while the exercise is practically the same every time it's done, the results are often startlingly different.

Preface

November 1986

Dear Sarah, Brian, Mary, and Mark,

As my offspring, I think it's important that you hear from me, not only the history of the Blue-Eyes/Brown-Eyes exercise, which caused you so much pain in your adolescence, but also why I thought it was so important that I kept on doing it even though it was causing that pain. I don't think I'm capable of writing a book for the world to read, or one which the world would choose to read, but I know I'm capable of writing a letter to all of you which will help you to understand what I did, even if you can't forgive me for doing it.

Sarah, you've been married and have lived in Saudi Arabia, a culture which is totally different from the one in which you were raised. Perhaps reading this letter to and with your children will help them to understand what's happening to them, when the racist behavior starts, as it surely will, both in SA and the good old U.S. of A., since you have experienced what our culture calls a 'mixed marriage.'

Brian, perhaps reading this will help you to understand that much of what happened to you at the hands of your peers, your teachers, and the coaches in Riceville was in reaction to me and what I had done, not because of something lacking in you. You've proven, in the way you've lived, that old adage that says, "The village dogs bark, but the caravan moves on."

Mary, you're in San Diego where diversity is the order of

the day. Perhaps reading this will help you to understand why you are so accepting and appreciating of those who are different from yourself. You and Mark were in classes in which some of your peers had gone through the exercise and, as you've told me, they understood what I had done better than Sarah's and Brian's classmates did, since none of them had experienced the exercise.

Mark, you're the one who's probably going to have the longest fallout from this whole thing, because you've opted to stay in the Riceville area. Your children will inevitably become associated with your mother, as long as we're both here. That's good news and bad news, as you've already learned. Someday they may read this letter, and gain some insights into the behaviors of those around them that they might not have gained otherwise.

Or, my dears, perhaps I may decide to have this whole thing printed and so reap some financial benefits from the barn dirt we've all experienced because of what's described here. If that happens, we'll all take a trip to Scotland and Ireland, since that's where we all came from, so long ago.

For several years I've been trying to think of a way to leave a record for you describing the inception, development, implementation, and results of the eye-color exercise in discrimination, which I first used in my third-grade classroom on the day after Martin Luther King Jr. was killed. The television documentaries and interviews, and the book, <u>A Class Divided</u>, by William Peters, don't tell the whole story, because each of them is only a fragment of the whole thing as seen through the eyes of someone else. I want you to know what happened as I experienced it.

I probably would have postponed this indefinitely but for

something that happened in a workshop in Denver last week. Sarah, you were there and will remember the tall, muscular, oval-faced, very fair-skinned man who delivered the impassioned tirade about the fact that we are all Americans, and that those of us who don't like the way America works can pack up and go back to where we came from. You were concerned about his attitude and behavior toward me, but I wasn't – until later in the day when I saw him as he came rushing back into the room after a break. We were going to show the film, "The Eye of the Storm." I was standing in the hall talking to one of the participants and as he passed behind her he grinned at me over her head. All I could see of him was that grin on his face. It was like seeing a disembodied death's head floating past and leering at me. Do you remember the scene in "Raiders of the Lost Ark" where they open the Ark of the Covenant and the German officer looks into the Ark and his face begins to disintegrate? That's what I saw when he leered at me. It was an eerie and a chilling feeling. I feel, now, a sense of urgency to get the information about the exercise down on paper so that you will have access to it should you want it in the future.

Numerous people have suggested that I write a book. I'm not an author. I am, however, the person who knows the most about this experience, so I am going to describe it as I saw it and you will be kind enough not to critique my writing too keenly.

December 11. 2015

OMG! Is this possible? Has it been 24 years since I started this thing? It seems like yesterday and yet…I honestly thought that there would come a time, in my lifetime, when describing this exercise for other people to read would be unnecessary. How wrong I was.

Acknowledgements

The students in the Riceville Community Schools and their parents, who didn't demand that I be fired; Superintendents Donald Johnston, Dean Weaver, and Norman Kolberg; Principals Dinsmore Brandmill, Leonard Crawford, and Steven Harnack; staff members Elaine Eschweiler and Eleanor Crawford; Riceville Recorder editor, M. E. Messersmith; photographer and friend, Charlotte Button; lawyer, advisor, and friend, Susan A. Golenbock; the facilitators at US West, US West Direct, and Public Service of Colorado; our family's dearest friend, Yvonne Tourtellott, and Resource Person Extraordinaire John Mans.

1 Don't Light a Fire You Can't Put Out

I actually used the Blue-Eyes/Brown Eyes exercise for the first time on April 5th, 1968, the day after Martin Luther King Jr. was killed. But the idea for it goes back to my days as an undergraduate student at Iowa State Teachers College in Cedar Falls, Iowa. It was there that I read <u>Mila 18</u>, by Leon Uris, and realized for the first time that eye color could be and had been used to determine whether people in a civilized society lived or died. On the weekends when I'd go home to the large, contentious, vocal Irish family into which I'd been born, we'd invariably get into spirited discussions of whatever weird ideas my five siblings and I had picked up during the week. We seemed usually to be at loggerheads with my father, when the subject was Race, and he would begin to lose the argument. His final statement would inevitably be, "If you don't like the way I think, you can always leave; the road's not crowded."

I'd go back to college shaking my head in despair because I'd discovered that my father, whom I idolized, had feet of clay. He was – is – the most honest man I've ever known. I think his father must have raised him on things like <u>Poor Richard's Almanac</u> because he was constantly quoting adages which to you may seem like clichés, but to him were words to live by. I couldn't possibly count the times I heard him say, "A fair thing's a pretty thing, and a right wrongs no man," and, "Never put a stone in another man's path."

How could a man who said he believed those things possibly be a racist? He was, and it bothered me a lot. I remember going back to school and discussing his racist attitudes with my roommate, Marilyn Alcorn, and saying, "If hazel eyes ever go out of style, my dad's in big trouble."

It was then that I realized how vulnerable we all are and how fragile our freedoms are: Anything could arbitrarily be chosen as the basis for discriminatory practices by those who wish to identify an enemy, or a victim, or who need someone to whom they can feel superior. I pondered how it would feel to live in a society where your very life depended on having the right color eyes, and I realized that there were lots of black people walking around in Waterloo, Iowa, only nine miles away, who could have described explicitly for me how it felt to have your life, and your children's lives, depend on having the right color skin.

In 1968, I was teaching third grade in Riceville, and we were involved in the Indian unit. I always taught the Indian unit in the spring of the year because by the end of April, the kids were getting pretty tired of the classroom. The grass was growing, the sap was rising, and the outdoors was beckoning to these nine year olds. I had to do something to make them eager to come back to school each morning.

Our lesson plan for April 5th was to learn the Sioux Indian prayer which says," Oh, Great Spirit, keep me from ever judging a man until I have walked a mile in his moccasins." We were all looking forward to putting up the tepee that my previous year's third-graders had made, sitting in it while we sang Indian songs (composed by white people), read Indian folk tales (written by white people), learned Indian poems (compiled by white people), and learned that wonderful Sioux Indian prayer (which Indians were saying before white people got here and taught them how to pray properly, and who to pray to). My plan for the evening was to wash and dry the tepee, then spread it out on the living room floor and iron it. First, however, I would get our four kids fed and watered and bedded down, and then I would watch television as I ironed and waited for Darald to come home from his second-shift job at the White Manufacturing plant, 25 miles away. As I walked into the house at end of the school day, that fateful Thursday, the telephone was ringing and, when I answered it, my sister Mary was on the other end and she said, "Is your television on?"

"No," I replied. "What's going on?"

"You'd better turn it on. They shot him."

"Who did they shoot, this time?" I asked in dread. You see, we'd already been through the assassination, in 1963, of John F. Kennedy, our first Catholic President, and the memory of his death was fresh in my mind. I was quite certain that no one would have the audacity, or the stupidity, to shoot another historical figure, in my lifetime.

"Martin Luther King," my sister replied.

As I write this, I get the same awful sensation in my gut and my eyes that I did that night. How could this be? Martin Luther King had been one of our "Heroes of the Month", in February, along with, unfortunately, George Washington, who owned slaves; Abraham Lincoln, who refused to free the slaves, until he was compelled to do so; Daniel Boone, who invaded and occupied the Indians' territory; and Davey Crockett, who was famous because he was killed as he tried to take over part of Mexico. None of these facts were included in the standard elementary curriculum at that time. And I'm not sure they are to this day.

I rushed to turn on the television, and then the horror not only became real; it intensified. The reactions and behaviors of the television reporters, on that ugly night were totally inexplicable. As I sat there I was struck by the insensitivity of the white male reporters who were interviewing leaders of the black community. As I remember it, Walter Cronkite asked three members of the black community, "When our leader was killed several years ago, his widow held us together. Who's going to keep your people in line?" Cronkite was one of my heroes and I couldn't believe that he would ask such an insensitive question. Was JFK the leader only of white people? Was MLK's message only relevant to black people? The fact that he would refer to the black community as 'your people,' I found extremely offensive. The idea that he believed white people were so civilized that a young woman could hold us together, but he couldn't imagine that anyone could keep the black community 'in line," was totally unacceptable. I was appalled at the seeming implication that "they" and "we" weren't part of the same society, that "our" leader (John F. Kennedy) was not "their" leader, and that the death of Martin Luther King Jr. was seen as a tremendous loss only to the black community.

In disgust, I changed the channel and there was Dan Rather asking three leaders of the black community, "Don't you negroes think that you should feel sympathy for us white people during this event because we can't feel the anger that you negroes can?" WHY WASN'T HE ANGRY? Did he not realize how insensitive and ignorant that question was?

If these erudite, sophisticated, intelligent adults hadn't recognized the racism in their own remarks, how could third graders in all white, all-Christian Riceville, Iowa possibly understand the true meaning of the racism in our society? I decided to give my students the opportunity not only to learn the

4

Sioux prayer, but to have it answered for them. I decided that on the following day we would talk about the death of Martin Luther King Jr. and, if my students didn't seem to understand the significance of this death, I was going to arrange for them to walk in another person's moccasins for one day.

I had read many books that described the Holocaust, when Hitler and his cohorts arrested, imprisoned, tortured, and killed over 10 million people before and during World War II, and I knew that one of the ways they decided who would be subjected to that treatment was eye color. If you had blue eyes, you could be a member of the Master Race: white, blond, blue-eyed Aryans who would rule the world. Anyone not fitting that description would be either killed or enslaved. These techniques worked during the Spanish Inquisition, when the target was the Jewish population. Hitler simply replicated their behaviors, when he came to power in 1933, to rid Europe of the Jewish population. It worked for the Nazis, and at the risk of being labeled a Nazi, I decided to use it with my third graders the next day.

I finished ironing the tepee, then rolled it up and shoved it into the closet in our bedroom. Instead of learning about Native Americans the next day, as directed in our standard curriculum, my students were going to find out how it feels to walk in the shoes of a child of color in this country. I was going to create a microcosm of society in my classroom by doing what those who run this show do every day. I was going to pick out a group of people on the basis of a physical characteristic over which they have no control. I was going to lower my expectations of those who had that physical characteristic. I was going to treat them as if all the things I was saying about them were in fact, true, and when they began to live down to my expectations of them, I was going to use their inadequate performance to prove that all the things I accused them of were real. And because eye color and skin color are caused by the same chemical, melanin, I chose eye color as the physical characteristic on which I would hang my lesson. After all, if it makes sense to judge people by the amount of melanin in their skin, it makes even more sense to judge them by the amount of melanin in their eyes, since our eyes are closer to our brains, and eye color, like skin color, is immutable.

In those few hours, I made a decision which was to change our lives, forever. I immediately began to map out the lesson plan for the next day. How should it begin? Should I wait until a student asked for an explanation of what had happened that day? Would the students really care about what had happened, since they had never met MLK? Would they be as upset as I was, or would it just be one more black man who was a trouble maker, and who got what he asked for, by trying to rock the boat in this society? Was I going to ask the principals' permission for what I was about to do? What if he refused to let me do what I thought needed to be done? What if I lost my job over this exercise?

By the time Darald got home, I had stopped crying, and swearing, and damning to Hell the whites who were on television sneering, and cheering, and waving their hoods and robes. I had become quietly determined that no student of any age would ever be allowed to express those attitudes or exhibit those behaviors in my presence; nor would they be willing to tolerate that kind of behavior from their peers. I was, and am, an educator, and it is my job to lead people out of ignorance. I knew then, and I know now, that treating people positively or negatively on the basis of the amount of a chemical in their skin is the height of ignorance. And the cure for ignorance is education, not indoctrination, or teaching, or training, but education.

When Darald walked in the door, he put down his lunch pail, held out his arms, and wrapped me up, and, with his chin resting on my head, said, "He was one of your Heroes of the Month, in February, wasn't he? How are you going to explain this to your students?"

Still holding tightly to the one who had been my rock for 13 years, I shook my head and said, "How can I explain something to them, that I don't understand, myself? There are no words to make sense of this for nine-year-olds. If I just pay lip-service to this ugliness, I'll be no better than the television anchors, who are indirectly accusing negroes of being savage and undisciplined, and the white Klan members and their supporters who are indicating that he should have stayed 'in his place.' He was in his place, Darald. He was peacefully demonstrating against prejudice and discrimination in order to show people a better way to bring about change. He wasn't rioting. He was marching for peace and freedom, not for money and fame. And look what being peaceful got him! They shot him, Darald. They shot Martin Luther King, Jr. They've killed hope. We moved out of Waterloo to escape this kind of thing, but there's no escaping the hatred and the ignorance of people who are being reinforced in the determination to hate negroes." By now, I was out of Darald's arms and warming up the leftover casserole and setting his place at the table.

"So, what are you going to do, tomorrow?" Darald asked, a little concerned.

"Our lesson plan for tomorrow was to learn the Sioux Indian prayer which says, 'Oh Great Spirit, keep me from ever judging a man until I have walked a mile in his moccasins.' But I'm not going to just teach them that prayer; I'm going to arrange to have it answered for them."

By this time, I was seated at the table next to him and I said, "Do you remember when we were living in Waterloo, in that little house on Littlefield Road and the National Tea Company decided to transfer you to Fort Dodge and we had to rent out our house? We knew they'd probably be transferring us back there, so I put an ad in the Waterloo Courier for a house for rent. Do you remember how disgusted with myself I was, when a woman called and asked me if we'd rent to 'coloreds'? I remember it as if it happened yesterday, I paused, and I can remember thinking of how angry the neighbors would be if we did that, and how tough it would be on our kids, and I said, 'This is an all-white neighborhood'. I knew immediately what I had done: I had forced her to make the decision because I was too chicken to do it. I had always sworn that I'd never cooperate with racism for any reason whatsoever. And, when the chips were down, I defected to the enemy. I'm not going to do that again, tomorrow."

"Well," Darald said, as he got up to put his dishes in the sink and put the milk into the refrigerator, "you were only dealing with one person who you'd probably never see again, and she knew what she had to do, and understood what you had to do. You aren't the first person who ever treated her like shit, and you won't be the last. This is Iowa in 1968, and Riceville is just like any other small town in this state. You'll never change these people, and you're going to get yourself into a lot of trouble with this thing. You'd better think it over. It's not just you and me we have to think about: These four kids are likely to have some really tough times, if you go ahead with this." He then told me that the men he rode to work with had made those typically ugly and obnoxious remarks on the way home, just like the remarks he had heard so often out of our white friends and his coworkers in Waterloo. Even though there were eight Christian churches in Riceville, that I'd ought to remember how some of our really religious neighbors in Waterloo would get up early on Sunday morning and drive all the way across town to a church on the east side, where they could get down on their knees and pray that their

8

kids wouldn't have to be bussed all the way across town to go to school with blacks.

As we turned off the television and got into bed, Darald pulled the blankets up around us, spooned into my back, and said, "Your dad told me there'd me times like this."

"Then why did you marry me?" I asked.

"Because he also told me there'd be times like this," Darald said, as he put his arm across my body.

He was quickly asleep, but I went to sleep repeating over and over one of the few prayers I've made a conscious effort to learn, "Lord, make me an instrument of thy peace. Lord, make me an instrument..." Had I known anything about racism I wouldn't have said that prayer that night and I probably wouldn't have done the eye-color exercise the next day. But I'm a liberal white female, and my number one freedom in this society is the freedom to be ignorant about racism and its effects. My number two freedom is the freedom to deny my own ignorance where racism is concerned. And my number three freedom is the freedom to tell people who accuse me of making racist remarks that they "just don't understand," or they "took it wrong," or they're "just too sensitive."

Had I known that my four offspring would be physically and verbally abused by their peers, their teachers, and the parents of their peers because their mother was what was called the town's "nigger lover", I probably wouldn't have done the exercise. Had I known that our family would lose most of our "friends" in Riceville because I taught that it was okay not to be white, I probably wouldn't have done the exercise. Had I known that my parents, who managed our small restaurant and hotel in Riceville, would lose their restaurant business because they had raised the town's "nigger lover," I probably wouldn't have done the exercise. However, had I known that I would be almost totally isolated by my fellow teachers in Riceville because none of them wanted to risk being accused of being like me – I probably would have done the exercise sooner! I found that I had a lot more time to teach when I was no longer included in their 'hall conferences', and my internal environment was a lot less polluted when I no longer had to listen to their racist, sexist, ageist, homophobic, ethnocentric remarks. But I didn't know about racism's effects, and I did do the exercise, and within fifteen minutes after I started the exercise that ugly Friday, I learned something extremely valuable: Be careful what you pray for, because you might get it, and you might discover that what you prayed for was exactly what you did not want.

2 "...to see ourselves as others see us."

I got up early the next morning, and as I was going out the door, leaving Darald to get the kids fed and off to school, he gave me that look, and said, "You know you could lose your job, by doing this thing, don't you?"

"Yes," I said. "I know that, but if I don't do something meaningful in answer to this ungodly event, I should lose my job. I know that just talking about what is going on where black people are concerned in this society, is absolutely unacceptable, and as an educator, it's my job to lead the students in my care out of the ignorance of racism." I was committed to doing this thing and after I did it, numerous people, including my mother, told me that I should have been committed for doing it.

"Then are you still determined to go ahead with your plan?" He asked.

"Is Martin Luther King still dead, this morning?" I snapped, and hurried out the door so that he wouldn't see the tears in my eyes.

The events of that day are chronicled in William Peters' book, A Class Divided, Then and Now. It's a quick and entertaining read, but it leaves out some important things that happened during that ugly day. So, at the risk of being repetitious, I'm going to describe the events of that day as I now recall them.

The first student who came into my room that morning was Steven Armstrong and, as he entered, he said, "Hey, Elliott! They shot that King, last night! Why'd they shoot that King?"

"We're going to talk about that, Steven," I replied, and after all the students were entered and seated, we did what had to be done the first thing in every school morning: We put our right hands over our hearts and said the Pledge of Allegiance to the flag of the United States of America, which was written in 1892, but had been amended in 1954, to include the words, 'under God.' We all knew that praying in school was a violation of the Constitution of the United States, but the Pledge was a tradition that we chose to perpetuate, just as we chose to perpetuate racism and all the other -isms which we so vigorously taught, and so vigorously decried. Then, as we usually did, we sang, "God Bless America." I was fully aware that we were, once again, violating the Constitution, but my students loved that song and voiced it with great enthusiasm, as usual. There's nothing like starting the day with a prayer.

"Good job," I said to the students as they settled back into their seats. Now, does anyone want to talk about what happened in Memphis, Tennessee, last night?" Every student raised his or her hand and started to demand why Martin Luther King had been shot. Their fathers had said some pretty awful things about the man who had been one of our heroes and the kids were confused as to who was right. Was I wrong, when I encouraged them to admire

MLK, or were their fathers wrong, when they criticized him?

It shortly became obvious to me that even though Martin Luther King had been one of our heroes of the month in February, and even though my students had been exposed to my liberal and enlightened philosophy for seven months, they still hadn't internalized anything they'd "learned" about brotherhood and respect for others. I asked them what they knew about Blacks and they mouthed every negative stereotype most of us have ever heard. I asked them how they knew those things were true and almost in unison they said, "'Cause my dad said so." I've asked that same question of practically every group of children with whom I've done the exercise, and each group has given that same response. Parents, be careful what kind of things you say around your children; they will go out and repeat what you say, and they will become what you are!

We then discussed integration of the schools and why the Negroes were demanding it. We discussed discrimination and segregation and all those other fine, valuable words, and ideas; and I could see that these kids weren't learning a damned thing; they were only doing what we white people have done in this country for at least the last 25 years: They were saying all the right things and not understanding a thing I was trying to teach, so with bated breath, I asked, "Do you kids have any idea how it would feel to be denied a job, or a house, or a good education, just because someone didn't like the color of your skin?"

"No, Mrs. Elliott," they all chorused.

"Would you like to do something, today, that will help you to find out how that would feel?" I asked.

"Yes, Mrs. Elliott, let's do that," they responded. It was obvious that they knew we'd already gotten out of reading and spelling, and, if they kept me talking, they wouldn't have to learn anything, all day long. You see, the learning activities that I usually planned for my students were fun and exciting, and this was bound to be just as pleasant as all the rest had been.

"Alright," I said. "In order to separate you into two groups, we're going to have to pick out something about you that is different from one another. Can you think of anything that we might use?"

"How about separating the boys and girls? That's something different and we can't change that," one child suggested.

"No, we do that in this school all the time, and I don't want to use something that you will be dealing with for the rest of the year," I replied.

"How about hair color?" one asked.

"Can't we change our hair color?" I asked.

"Oh, yeah, my mother dyes her hair all the time." one brave soul said.

"Yeah, you never know what color her hair is going to be," another agreed.

"We can't use height, because you're the only tall one in the class, Mrs. Elliott," one student offered. They suggested weight, but that's something that we can change.

How about our clothes? Nope, we change those every day, so that won't work. How about having some of us wear a ribbon, or a sign of some kind? No, we could take those off. Finally, one of the quieter students said,

"How about eye color? You told us that eye color and skin color are caused by the same chemical, so why don't we use that?"

Immediately they were all in total agreement, and I said, "All right. Today, we're going to judge people by the color of their eyes, and since most of the students in this room are blue-eyed, the brown-eyed children will be on top the first day."

"What do you mean?" David asked.

"I mean, that today brown-eyed people are going to be the better people in this room. Brown-eyed people are smarter than blue-eyed people. They are cleaner than blue-eyed people, and they are more civilized than blue-eyed people," I replied.

Immediately, brown-eyed Debbie, sitting in the front row, demanded, "How come you're the teacher, here? You've got them blue-eyes."

Taken aback, and frankly, not knowing what to say, I paused, and in an instant Alan, from the back row, spoke up in my defense, "If she didn't have them blue-eyes, she'd be either the principal or the superintendent. They're both brown-eyed," he announced. And thus began the first real learning for the day. I couldn't believe how quickly my students began to exhibit all the language and behaviors that are characteristic of bigots. Why was it so easy for them to come up with these criticisms of their peers, students who had been their best friends, only minutes before?

I quickly told all the blue-eyed children to move their desks to the back rows of the room and asked the brown-eyed children to move the desks to the front of the room. The Browns did the task with extreme enthusiasm, while the Blues dragged their feet and their desks to the back of the room, as they had been directed to do.

Once the room was re-arranged, I said, "Now, you blue-eyed children are going to have to wear an armband so that I can tell what color your eyes are, without having to get too close to you." I had cut ugly drab green construction paper into strips and I now commenced to wrap one around the upper right arm of each blue-eyed child. The expressions on the faces of those children, as that ugly symbol of their inferiority was pinned into place, were utterly indescribable. Lesson number two, for the day: How do good Christians manage to maintain their abuse of those who are different from themselves every day? Do they deny that it's happening? Do they pretend that they don't see what effect their unkindness has on those 'others'? How do we justify perpetuating this injustice?

From the first moment of that awful day, I watched my brown-eyed students become people that I scarcely knew. When a blue-eyed child didn't practice the listening skills, a brown would say it was because of his eye-color. When a blue-eyed boy, who had been the class favorite, only moments before, made a mistake on his spelling paper, it was blamed on his eye-color. When a blue-eyed boy ran in the hall, it was because, 'That's the way they are.' When a blue-eyed girl didn't have a sharpened pencil it was, "Well, she's a Bluey."

When I, the heretofore beloved teacher pulled down the roller map, the ring slipped off my finger and the map wrapped around and around the roller, with that ugly, flapping sound, and I said, "Well, I've done it again," expecting, of course, for all the students to understand, since that happened quite frequently. Not so! Brown-eyed Debbie, sitting in the front row had obviously been waiting to get me all year, for it took not a second for her to say, "Well, whaddaya expect? You've got blue eyes haven'cha?" I was furious, and for just an instant, in my mind's eye, I could see myself backhanding that little brown-eyed bitch against the wall. I wanted her to hit the wall and slide down like a broken egg, and I wanted to be at the bottom of the wall, when she got there. I had never thought that way about a student, before, and only one, since. I was angry at Debbie, but I quickly became even more angry at myself! What was I thinking of? This innocent child was exhibiting the behaviors and using the language she had learned from people like me. This didn't suddenly spring out of a vacuum in her mind; this had been a part of her conditioning since birth. She wasn't saying anything unique; this was the way she had heard adults like me respond to the mistakes made by those 'others' all her life. "That's the way they are." And, "They're all alike." And, "Give them something nice, and they'll just wreck it." And, "You can always tell a Norwegian, (or Polack, or Spic, or Nigger, or Wop, or Jap), but you can't tell 'em much." And the all-too-familiar, "Would you want your daughter to marry one?"

My own father had cautioned my two sisters and me, when we were in high school, not to date those handsome and charming brothers, whom everyone adored, because their grandmother was an octoroon and we'd run the risk of having black children, and, as he put it, "I don't want any pick-a-ninnies in my grandchildren."

All of this came charging back into my mind as I looked at that little girl, sitting there with a satisfied smirk on her face and challenging me to correct her. She seemed to be thinking, "You asked for this; now, what are you going to do about it?"

Before I could utter a word, blue-eyed Alan, in the back row, said, "Aw, Debbie, her eyes ain't got nothin' to do with it; you know she never has been able to do that right." I didn't correct Debbie for what she'd said and I didn't correct Alan for speaking so disparagingly of me. I thanked him for defending me, fully realizing that he wasn't sticking up for me because I was his teacher: He was defending me because his eye color was the same as mine, and if my eye color made me inferior, then his eye color, which was the same as mine could make him inferior, too, and he couldn't allow that to happen.

In that short exchange, I learned more than I have ever learned in a short time, before or after that day. I learned about the anger of being judged as less competent, less intelligent, and less deserving of justice, simply because of a physical characteristic over which we have no control. Is this what happens to black children in the schools and churches and grocery stores and theatres on a daily basis, in the 'land of the free and the home of the brave'? I learned about the despair of knowing the situation is rigged against you and there's nothing you dare do about it. I learned what being 'damned with faint praise' really means. I learned something about how it feels to have your status, your educational level, your social standing, your position of power, totally ignored, because of a physical characteristic which, until that moment, had been totally insignificant to you, and to others.

Debbie's simple question shouldn't have affected me so strongly; I knew this was an exercise and that she probably was only pretending to judge me unfairly. But that didn't keep me from reacting to her words and her attitude. What must it be like to be exposed to that kind of treatment every day and to know that you'd better not do what Alan did? People get shot for defending the 'others' in this society, fairly consistently.

After thanking Alan for his defense, I quickly tried to get back to 'business as usual.' But there was no going back. As the students continued their daily lessons in reading, writing and arithmetic, I observed some obvious, and undeniable, differences: Brown-eyed, dyslexic boys, who had been unable to deal adequately with printed language symbols, suddenly were working at a higher level than they ever had before, in my room. I had seven dyslexic boys in the room, that year, and four of them were brown-eyed. On the day they were on the top in that exercise, they read words I knew they couldn't read and they spelled words I knew they couldn't spell. At the end of the day, brown-eyed Billy came up to my desk and said, "Where's my spelling paper, Mrs. Elliott?"

"What do you want it for, Billy?" I asked.

"I wanna take it home and show it to my mother. She thinks I can't spell, and I can." He had tears in his eyes, as did I, in mine. What had we done to this kid and his older brother, over the years? Oh, my God! How many children had I failed to reach, up to this point?

On the other hand, in the space of one day, I watched bright, ambitious, eager blue-eyed children become timid, intimidated, insecure, angry little people in the space of a few minutes. Carol, the Lutheran minister's daughter, had come into my room in February, reading at the sixth-grade level. She had a steel trap mind, could attain and retain information like no child I had ever encountered before. She had never learned how to multiply, so I spent the first fifteen minutes of math class teaching her the basics of third-grade multiplication. She never made a mistake in multiplication until the day she had the wrong color eyes. On that day she made mistakes in reading and spelling, and she forgot how to multiply! I watched that child disintegrate before my very eyes. She stumbled when she walked across the classroom; she walked with her shoulders hunched, as if to ward off an expected blow, and she came in from recess, crying.

"What's going on here?" I asked, after recess, when all the students were back in their seats. The students agreed that, as Carol walked across the playground, two brown-eyed Cindys, and brown-eyed Debbie stepped up behind her. Debbie struck her across the back with her forearm and, when Carol turned around to confront her, Debbie said, "Now you have to apologize to me for gettin' in my way, 'cause I'm better'n you are." And Carol apologized and came in crying. I was furious. Carol was crushed. And Debbie was defiant and triumphant. She had both Carol and me in a vise, and she knew it. She was doing exactly what she had been programmed to do; treat others unfairly on the basis of a physical characteristic over which they have no control and defy the authority figure to do anything about it. Her body language, her words, and her facial expression all said the same thing: You started this thing; now, what are you going to do about it?

What was I going to do about it? I couldn't just call the whole thing off, because that would destroy the reality that I had tried to create with the exercise. When are we going to call off racism, in this country? I couldn't take Debbie and her friends aside and chastise them; when have we ever satisfactorily punished white miscreants for the damage they do to people of color every day? How often have we seen white people abuse, mistreat, even kill, people of color and not be properly punished for it? I did what we white folks do: I tried to explain to Carol that Debbie was being ignorant and unfair, and that she was the one who was wrong, not Carol. I used the old, "Sticks and stones may break my bones, but names will never hurt me," and the ever popular, but not powerful, piece of advice to 'show that you're a better person than s/he is,' as if that would help, or would stop it from happening again the minute I turned my back. Did that help? Hell, no! And it didn't wipe that smirk off Debbie's face, nor change the strut with which she walked across the classroom.

That was the worst day I had ever spent in the classroom. I wanted to call the whole thing off. By lunchtime, I had decided that I had to put a stop to this craziness, but I needed to hear what my peers would do in this situation. So I went down to the teachers' lounge to get some advice and support from the other two third-grade teachers. They, and several other teachers were in the lounge, and I tried to tell them what was happening in Room 10. Big mistake! When I had finished describing the morning's events, the younger of the two said, in response to what I had experienced, "I don't know how you have time for all that extra stuff; it's all I can do to teach reading, writing, and arithmetic." Well, in my estimation, she hadn't done a great job of educating in those areas, so she might as well have done 'all that extra stuff.'

The other third-grade teacher, who was over sixty years old, and had been molding young minds for over thirty years, said, in response to what I had described, "I don't know why you're doing that. I thought it was about time somebody shot that son-of-a-bitch." I was shocked and appalled at her words. How could she say such a thing? She was a devout Christian! She couldn't be serious? I waited for a reaction to her words from the other professionals in the room, and it wasn't long in coming. Not one of my peers said, "Do you realize what you've just said?" Or, "Judge not that ye be not judged." Or, "Do unto others as you would have others do unto you." Or, "God is love." Or, "Insomuch as ye have done it unto one of these, my brethren, so have ye done it unto me." Or, "Do you realize that you could lose your job, for saying that in this building?" I looked around that small room, full of educated women, and every one of them was either smiling or laughing, and nodding. Had she expressed their feelings perfectly and, as the oldest member of the group, had the most right to do so? Or was the laughter nervous laughter in shame at what she had been so bigoted as to say? I want to give them the benefit of the doubt, now, but at that time all I could do was stumble out of that room and back to my classroom, determined to finish the day as it had begun: no student of any age will ever leave my presence with those attitudes unchallenged. I may not be able to change peoples' attitudes, but I can challenge them. Those who would excuse someone shooting another human being, just because they were protesting the kind of treatment that blacks were getting in this country at that time, are wrong.

Just think about it: if my students reacted in these ways after only one day of being judged unfairly on the basis of the amount of melanin in their eyes, what if, not only you, but your parents, your grandparents, your teachers, your friends, your enemies, the policeones, the fireones, the doctors, the ministers, the garage mechanics, the scoutmasters, all the significant adults and all the children in your environment, had become convinced of the validity of judging human beings by the amount of melanin in their eyes? Or in their hair? Or in their skin?

And that, after all, is the problem, isn't it? Many whites in this country, then, and today, don't see people of color as entirely human. They don't realize that we are all members of the same race; not the black race, or the white race, or the yellow race, or the red race. Those are all simply color groups. We are all members of the HUMAN race, and are all descendants of those common ancestors; black women who evolved at or near the equator, from 140,000 to 280,000 years ago. Therefore, it's going to be very difficult for you to prove to me that white people are superior to people of color, because we are all members of the same race, and melanin, the chemical that gives our skin its color, does not affect our intelligence, or our worth as human beings. I believe that the anger, distrust, and hatred that we see between white people and people of color in this country would never have happened if white folks hadn't deliberately introduced, and acted upon, racism based on skin color in what has become the United States of America.

Now, if you don't learn anything else from reading this material, learn this: There is no gene for Racism! You were not <u>born</u> a racist! You were, however, born into a racist society, and have lived in it since your birth. Racism is not instinctive; it is a learned response. Realize that anything you learn you can unlearn. You can rid yourself of your racism.

As I watched my students become what I, and the other significant adults in their environment, had taught them to be, I suddenly remembered the line in a Robert Burns' poem, which says, "If some great power the gift could give us, to see ourselves as others see us." I got that opportunity that day, and I've never forgotten it. If people of color see us white folks the way I saw my brown-eyed students that day, we whites have no right to expect their respect.

We finished the day with the browns on top and the blues on the bottom, and, since it was Friday, I was certain the kids would 'get over it' by Monday morning. However, my learning was not to stop so suddenly. I was afraid to go home; I was sure my telephone would be ringing off the wall as parents and/or administrators called to demand to know what I had done to my students that day. I was certain there'd be a cross burning in my front yard. I was sure that all Hell was going to break loose and

I'd have to deal with it alone, since Darald wouldn't be home for several hours. So I went uptown to the hotel that Darald and I owned and that my mother was managing. As I told her what was happening in my classroom, she listened attentively, but it was obvious that she thought I was more than a little hysterical. What I was describing sounded more like Orwell's 1984 than like Elliott's 1968, and she was apparently uncomfortable with what I was saying.

She said, "You'd better be careful, Jane. You don't want to end up where Aunt Eunice did."

"Where'd she end up?" I asked.

"In a mental institution," my mother replied. My mother actually thought that what I was describing sounded insane! And why wouldn't it sound insane? I had created a microcosm of society in my classroom for a day, and indeed, it did sound insane.

It is not rational to treat people positively or negatively on the basis of the amount of a chemical in their skin. To do so is to deny reality and live with a false sense of superiority or inferiority, and to try to force a lie to become the truth by constructing a myth to support your fallacious reasoning and unacceptable behaviors. It takes years of this indoctrination to maintain the power of the majority group, in this situation.

When I did go home I found yet another surprise awaiting me: No parent or administrator or student called me to complain about what I had done with the children on that day. Did the children complain to the parents, who either didn't listen or didn't believe them? Did the students not tell their parents about what they'd gone through during that distressing day? Did the parents hear about it and disapprove, but feel powerless to do anything about it? Did the students feel that what happens in the school world was irrelevant to what happens in the "real" world and so decide simply to leave the whole thing where it happened? If students can leave something as traumatic as this experience in school, what do they do with what they learn in math, social studies, reading and science, and in values clarification and sex education classes? What about their learning in catechism and other religion classes? It was a puzzling conclusion to a dilemma-filled day and I was glad to see it end. I was not so anxious for the weekend to pass, because that would force me to face Monday. I waited in worry and wonder.

I couldn't wait to tell Darald what had transpired during the day. It all sounded a little too far out, for him. He indicated that, if it had been as I was describing, we'd better be prepared to move out of town, because the 'boys' on the second shift had made it plain that they'd have no 'nigger lovers' in their community.

"You've probably thrown a monkey wrench into the works, Jane, and they aren't going to like having to deal with what you've started. These people are happy as they are; they haven't lived in a place like Waterloo, where there are lots of different kinds of people; they are here because they don't want to deal with those differences. You'd better fix this on Monday and hope it doesn't go any farther. We can't afford to move, right now, and these kids of ours like living close to their grandparents. Just leave it alone."

Little did we know that there was no 'fixing it.'
And there was definitely no leaving it alone, but we soon
found out what being left alone could feel like.

3 A Little Learning is a dangerous Thing

November, 1994

Well, Kids, so much for that "sense of urgency" I
felt in 1986. It's now eight years later and I'm finally back
to working on this project.

I went back into the classroom on Monday morning
dreading what I was going to do to my students, but
knowing that it had to be done, if the brown-eyed students
were going to learn some of what their blue-eyed peers had
learned on Friday. We almost immediately reversed the
exercise, putting the blue-eyed people on the top and
Browns on the bottom. The same kinds of things
happened on Monday as had on Friday – with one big, and
I think, significant difference; the Blues were much less
vicious to the Browns than the Browns had been to them. I
was relieved and pleased, but puzzled. What was going
on? Had they realized that it was all just a game? Had
they decided that it didn't mean anything? Or had they
learned something on Friday about the pain caused by
discrimination? I didn't know the answer, but at 2:30
when I told them to remove the armbands which the
inferior group members had been required to wear, I found
out, as the students embraced one another, grinned, cried a
little, and freely communicated for the first time in 2 days
of school, just what our society could be like if we

practiced what we preach. When the exercise was over the students were overjoyed to be together. It was as though we'd all become members of one extended family. It was absolutely amazing.

On Tuesday, before we'd discussed the exercise at all, I asked each student to write a four-paragraph composition telling what discrimination is, how the child felt on Friday, how the child felt on Monday, and who Martin Luther King Jr. was. After everyone had finished writing, we got in a circle and, if they wanted to, each child could share her/his essay with the group. Everyone was eager to share what he/she had written. The essays and the accompanying discussion were astounding and the learning was terrific.

Anyone reading their essays can learn a great deal...

"Discrimination means judging people by the color of their skin.

On Friday I felt happy because the people with brown eyes got to do everything first and we got five extra minutes of recess. I felt sad for the people with the blue eyes because they got to do everything last. On Monday I felt mad and I wanted to tie the people with blue eyes up and quit school because they got to do everything first and we had to do everything last. I felt dirty. And I did not feel as smart as I did on Friday. Discrimination is no fun. Martin Luther King didn't like discrimination against negroes." Debbie Anderson

"Discrimination means not liking a person because of the color of their skin.

Our room heard about when Martin Luther King died ad we wanted to see what it felt like to be a negro child, with black skin. The brown eyed children we the whites and the blue eyed children with the negroes. This was Friday. I have brown eyes. I was happy. The brown eyed children were hot shots; I felt good.

On Monday I felt mad because I was being discriminated against. The blue eyed people got to be first in line and the teacher just explained to the blue eyes their mistakes and bawled us brown eyes out. I was sick.

Martin Luther King was a negro preacher who believed that negro people should have the same right as white people. He died because of this." Sindee Hockens

"Discrimination is happy and not happy.

On Friday I felt good because I had brown eyes and we got to be row leaders and we got to sit any place in lunch. The blue eyed people had to be the unlucky ones and they were mad.

On Monday I could have locked them in jail because I was so mad.

The blue eyes got to be first in lunch line, and got to be first in lunch, and got five minutes extra of recess.

I didn't want to work. I didn't feel

like a was very big.

Discrimination is not fun at all. I am glad I am not a negro and being judged by my skin." Dale Brunner

"Discrimination means to be treated badly and judged by the color of your skin.

On Friday we practiced discrimination. The brown eyed boys and girls got to do what they wanted to do. I am brown eyed and the blue eyed boys and girls had to do what we wanted. I felt good inside.

On Monday we had the blue eyed people do what they wanted to do. I felt like I was going to tie all the blue eyed in the corner. I am brown eyed so I felt like crying.

Martin Luther King died trying to save colored people from discrimination. White people at least could treat colored people like any other person." Billy Thompson

"Discrimination is when people judge you by the color your skin is or he color your eyes are.

Last Friday the people in Mrs. Elliott's room who had brown eyed got to discriminate against the people who had blue eyes. I have brown eyes. I felt like hitting them if a wanted to. I got to have five minutes extra of recess. And when we went to reading class we could sit wherever we wanted to.

On Monday, April 8 the blue eyes got to discriminate against the people who had brown eyes. And I have brown eyes. I felt like quitting school. The blue eyed people got to do everything that we got to on Friday. But they got to have recess on Monday and we didn't. I felt made. That's what it feels when you're discriminated against. I won't ever discriminate against people again.

Martin Luther King died because he believed that negroes shouldn't be discriminated against." Debbie Hughes

"Discrimination means not liking people who have different colored skin. On Friday we practiced discrimination. The brown eyed people got to do things first. I have blue eyes. I felt like slapping a brown eyed person. It made me mad. Then I felt like kicking a brown eyed person. I felt like quitting school. The brown eyed people got five extra minutes of recess.

On Monday I was happy. I felt big and smart. Then we got 5 extra minutes of recess. We got to do everything first. And we got to take out the play ground equipment. I do not like discrimination. It made me sad. I would not like to be angry all my life." Theodore Perzynski

"On Friday, April 5, we had Discrimination Day. The people with brown eyes could do almost anything. The people with blue eyes could not do half the things the people with brown eyes did. I felt left out because I have blue eyes. I felt like giving them all black eyes.

On Monday, April 8, we had Discrimination Day again only the people with blue eyes got to be the wheels. Boy, was that fun! We got to do all the things first. That was living it up. I felt like I was smarter, bigger, better, and stronger."
Dennis Runde

"Discrimination is being judged by the color of your skin or the color of your eyes the church you go to. We wanted to find out how it felt to be discriminated against because of the color of your eyes.

On Friday we had the brown eyed people get to be the smarter ones and the blue eyed people were the negroes. I had blue eyes.; The brown eyed people got be first, got to drink out of the water fountain, got to bring our the toys, got to do the fun things, and to have more recess. I felt mad because I felt like I was left out. This was practicing discrimination. The brown eyed people were happy because they were the lucky ones.

On Monday I was very happy. The brown eyed people felt sad because they felt like they were left out. I felt happy because the blue eyed people were the smart ones.

Martin Luther King was killed because he was trying to help the negroes.

He died trying to help stoop discrimination. He was a preacher." Julie Kleckner

"On Friday I felt real sad and left out. The brown eyed people in room 10 for to play with the toys and the blue eyed people didn't. I have green eyes. I could have cried because the brown eyed people got to play with the phones and we didn't and we didn't get to drink out of the fountain, and didn't get to work on the teepee. I felt like crying, and being a drop out, and tieing the brown eyed people up.

On Monday I was happy because we discriminated against the brown eyed people and I felt smarter and gooder, and cleaner than the brown eyed people. Discrimination is bad. That's what I think because discrimination is sad and unhappy." Kim Reynolds

" Discrimination is a word for when a person is judged not by what he does but the color of his skin. I found out what it feels like in school.

On Friday, April 5, the people with brown eyes did everything first. The rest did everything last. They got to take out things to play with and the rest didn't. And I was a blue eyed person. And did I get mad. Why, I felt like never coming back to school!

But on Monday April 8, the blue eyed people did everything first. We could take out things to play with. We did things we couldn't do on Friday. Then I didn't feel sad. I felt very happy then.

Martin Luther King wanted negroes to have what they wanted just as white people do. And he was killed for doing this. He was killed by discrimination."
Carol Anderson

"Discrimination means judging a man by the color of his skin.

Friday we practiced discrimination. Friday the brown eyed people got to do what they wanted to do and Monday blue eyed people got to do what they wanted to do. I have blue eyes. Friday I wanted to hit the brown eyed people. I felt mad Friday. But Monday, I didn't mind that. We got to have five more minutes of recess. And you even got to go outside even if we didn't have our work done. But I don't like discrimination because I know how it feels." Alan Moss

"Discrimination is being judged by your skin color.

On Friday the people with brown eyes got to have a recess and art and I have brown eyes. I was happy. We did the same things on Monday except the blue eyes got to have long recess and p.e. and I felt like blowing the teacher sky high."
Bruce Fox

The first thing that we concluded as we shared those essays was that the way many women and members of other minorities behave is not because of a weakness peculiar to their genes. We had caused those same behaviors in white male and female students simply by arbitrarily accusing them of inferior status based on the color of their eyes!

We soon concluded that the anger seen in people of color is not because of their color, but is, instead, a reaction to the treatment they receive from white people who are uncomfortable with people whose color is different from their own. If you were treated every day as we had treated the "inferior" group each day of this exercise, might you become angry at those who were mistreating you?

We learned about violence. Almost every student stated that she/he wanted to do physical damage to the teacher and to the members of the abusive group. Why didn't they? Because it was an exercise and they'd agreed to go along with it. What would they do if they knew it was never going to end? Would they be willing to go along? No! If their lives were endangered because they'd refused to go along? They weren't so sure.

We learned something about drop-outs. The students agreed that they wouldn't be interested in coming to school if they knew they'd be mistreated on the basis of their eye color every day. Even if graduating from school meant the difference between getting a job in the future, or being unemployed? They weren't so sure.

We learned that you don't have to have people of color in your community to have racism. My students knew all those negative things about Blacks even though there were only white people in Riceville. Where had that knowledge come from, since there were no Blacks for them to observe? What was really the problem?

We learned that you aren't born a racist. You are taught to be a racist by the society in which you live. My students had no bias where those with a different eye color than their own were concerned until I imposed it upon them. We also learned that you can choose not to believe the lesson.

We learned that prejudice doesn't cause discrimination; discrimination causes prejudice. Pick out a group of people on the basis of a physical characteristic over which they have no control; assign negative traits to them because of that characteristic; treat them unfairly and, when they begin to react with anger and frustration to that treatment, castigate them for their behavior and blame their behavior on the physical characteristic instead of on your treatment of them. Discipline them for trying to defend their reactions, and for seeking a remedy to the treatment, and thereby prove to all those who witness the exchange that the "inferior" group members are argumentative, uncooperative, intractable, irrational people who don't appreciate the good things we are doing for them.

We learned about responsibility. We discovered that each of us helped to make the exercise work. It wouldn't have succeeded if most of the members of the "superior" group hadn't cooperated with the authority figure in the situation.

On the other hand, we learned about powerlessness. If the "inferior" group had refused to cooperate, it would simply have proven the validity of all our claims about them. Conversely, their passivity reinforced the descriptions of them as being weak and cowardly. If they had resisted physically they would have been accused of – and been punished for – being violent. The fact that they didn't could be used to prove that they were like sheep who, dumb and silent, could be led to the slaughter.

We learned about name-calling. Which of us had never heard, "Sticks and stone may break my bones but names will never hurt me"? It's not true. Words, someone has said, are the most powerful weapon devised by humankind. This exercise was conducted in language, and the pain resulted from speech. We told people they were superior or inferior and they reacted to what we said.

We spent most of that day debriefing and trying to put what we'd learned into perspective. Each of us found some way that what we'd experienced applied to something we'd seen, heard, said, or done at some time in the past. It was probably the most productive day I've ever spent in the classroom. I was reluctant to send the children home, that afternoon. In the past I had experienced days where the learning environment was so fun for them, my students didn't want to leave. Today's experience had brought us so close, they were even more reluctant to leave than usual.

After school I took the essays to the hotel and showed them to my mother. She asked to keep them overnight and showed them to the editor of the local paper. He asked if he could print them in the paper. That wasn't a problem for me; there are no secrets in my room, other than what students tell me in confidence. I, however, asked my students about having their essays printed. It was no problem for them; they thought everyone should know what they'd learned. Besides, they thought it would be exciting to have their essays in the paper. It turned out that we didn't know how exciting it would be!

Shortly after our essays appeared in the paper we got a call from Johnny Carson asking me to come in and discuss our "Discrimination Day" exercise on the Tonight Show. The kids were unimpressed. We had written letters to Coretta Scott King expressing our sorrow at the death of her husband and when the school secretary told us there was a long-distance call for me, the kids were sure it must be Mrs. King. When I called them on the intercom from the principal's office to tell them it was Johnny Carson calling, they said, "Who's Johnny Carson?"

The Carson show was my first experience on television. What an initiation! The first thing I was told during the pre-show was, "Don't say anything thought-provoking. The people who watch the Johnny Carson show don't want to think." The second thing they told me was, "Don't say anything depressing. The people who watch the Johnny Carson show don't want to be depressed."

I said, "Then why am I here? I can't think of anything that isn't depressing about racism."

John Carsey, who was interviewing me, said, "Don't worry. We're going to punch it up."

"Well," I said, "I'll stay then. I've never seen racism 'punched up'."

I stayed. We didn't "punch up" racism, but I learned a lot about Johnny Carson's audience. Over thirty percent of the letters I got after that show were so vicious and obscene that I didn't want to share them with my students. I didn't share the worst of them. On the other hand, the other letters were so appreciative and warm and thoughtful that they really helped to get me through some of the unpleasantness that followed.

4 Some Grow Older, Some Grow Up

During the following summer a member of the
Rotary Club in a nearby community called me and asked if
I'd be their luncheon speaker during one of the coming
weeks. Now bear in mind that at that time, women weren't
allowed to join the Rotary, but if we had done something
significant, amusing, or bizarre, we might be invited to
entertain them. Being on the Johnny Carson show must
have met one or more of those criteria so I was invited into
their presence. My having done the exercise wasn't
significant, amusing or bizarre enough, but having been on
the Carson show was? Naturally I found this a bit
ludicrous so I suggested that the person who was inviting
me might consider putting the Rotarians through the Blue-
eyed, Brown-eyed Exercise. Mr. Rotary was delighted and
we commenced to discuss how we'd set up the room and
conduct the exercise.

On the Wednesday of my visit to the Rotary, he
and I separated the men as they came through the door,
sent the Blues to stand over against the wall, let the
Browns fill their plates at the cafeteria line and then seat
themselves at the tables which had been set up for them at
the front of the room. The tables for the Blues were still
folded and stacked against the wall, as were their folding

chairs. There was a large roll of white paper standing there which they were to use to cover their tables, once they got them set up.

After all the Browns had been served, I instructed the Blues to get themselves in line and fill their plates. While they were filling their plates, a short, young, brown-eyed man in slightly soiled suntans came through the door. He was obviously one of the service station managers. I immediately handed him a plate, took him by the arm and told him to come with me, that he could go to the head of the line, since he had brown eyes. I then stopped the blue-eyed man who had just gotten the mashed potatoes dipped onto his plate and told him that he was to back up and let this brown-eyed man go ahead of him. At that point the blue-eyed man, who was about six feet tall, rather portly, and wearing a blue suit, white shirt, and red tie, took a half-step back and growled at me, "Lady, whaddya think you're doing?"

I responded by telling him that this man was better than he was and that he should move back and let the better man in.

At this, Bluey growled menacingly, "Lady, if my potatoes get cold while you're messin' around…"

To which I responded by placing my forearm against his considerable paunch and saying, "Look, don't blame me for the color of your eyes. Go talk to your mother about that. But in the meantime, get back and let this man in front of you," as I pushed against his paunch. I heard a sharp intake of breath above my head, and as I looked up the man's face seemed to swell like one of those African blowfish you see on the Discovery channel. My first thought was, "My God, he's going to hit me!" He didn't; he backed up and the little brown-eyed man filled his plate and went truckin' on down to join his brown-eyed friends in the positions of power at the front of the room. After the Browns had finished eating, and their tables had been cleared by the kitchen staff, the chairone rose and announced that the Blueys were to clear their own tables. At that the Blues held up a huge banner which they had made of the paper tablecloth material (You know how Blues are; they didn't recognize what paper is for, and they'll write on every clean surface they find.) on which they had written: "Elliot Go Home!" They misspelled Elliott, but someone helped them with 'go' and 'home'. The chairone repeated his request that they clear their tables, so they complied with his request by picking up the tables and carrying them over to the cafeteria counter and leaving them there to be cleared by the kitchen help.

The chairone then introduced me and I opened my remarks by saying, "Well, you can see that blue-eyed people aren't as civilized as brown-eyed people; they don't even know how to clear tables." At this, most of the blue-eyed boys got up and headed for the door.

As the first of them reached the doorway I said, "Oh, blue-eyed boys are alright. But you wouldn't want your daughter to marry one." Half of the group stormed through the door and didn't come back. Most of those who stayed were there past the one o'clock hour when Rotary Club luncheons usually ended and the last members left at about 2:30 PM.

That encounter took place in the summer of 1968. A few years after that encounter, our family moved to that community and purchased a business there. In 1992 Darald was to be inducted into a fraternal organization in that community. He and I were invited to a card party at which we were being introduced to the members of the group. I was seated at a card table as they were being introduced to me and this tall, white-haired older man came toward the table. As he approached the table the one making the introductions said, "Mrs. Elliott, this is Mr. K. K., this is Mrs. Elliott, Darald's wife." Mr. K. stopped dead in his tracks about eight feet from me, raised his arm, pointed his forefinger at me and, shaking it in agitation, said loudly,

"I know exactly who you are! I've never forgotten you and I've never forgiven you either."

Perplexed, I asked, "What's going on here? What have I done?"

Still shaking his finger at me the gentleman nearly shouted, "I'm blue-eyed!"

Now it was my turn to point a finger and as I did so, laughingly, I responded, "And you're a Rotarian!"

"Yes!" he shouted, "And I've never forgotten what you did to us that day!"

"But, Mr. K.," I said, "That was over twenty years ago. You can't still be angry about something that happened twenty years ago."

"I've never forgiven you and I never will," Mr. K. growled, and he stomped off to join a group in the far end of the room. To the day he died, that white male was angry about being treated unfairly for forty minutes, twenty years ago, on the basis of the color of his eyes. Those who have trouble understanding the anger in the communities of people of color in this country need to think about that. I know I thought of it every time I saw him and I'm sure he thought, too, every time he saw me. We thought about the same thing, but probably not in the same way.

5 Canadians Aren't Kidding

Something else interesting happened concerning the exercise that summer. Stephen Banker, a freelance television producer for the Canadian Broadcasting Company, called me and asked if I intended to do the Blue-eyed, Brown-eyed exercise during the coming school year. He had seen me describing it on the Johnny Carson show or something and thought it would make a good television documentary. I told him that I would be doing it but that he would have to get permission from the school administration to do any filming in my classroom. He got the permission and we planned the exercise for the third week in October. I wanted to get the exercise in early in the year so that we could build on what we learned, the previous year, for a longer time in my classroom. I also thought that, if the increased ability to learn which I thought I had seen in my students that first year, was not a coincidence, I wanted to create that advantage for them as early as possible.

We got a rather nasty surprise when parents came to register their children for school that August; twenty percent of the parents whose children were coming into third grade told the principal that they didn't want their children placed in "Elliott's classroom." This had never happened before, to my knowledge. Upon closer questioning of those who made this demand the principal discovered that they didn't want their children to learn what I was teaching about "them niggers."

Every year after that, the same thing occurred. Sometimes a parent, usually a father, would call and tell the principal not to "put my kid in that nigger lover's classroom," and the principal never had to say, "Which nigger-lover do you mean?" We all knew there was only one.

I'll never forget the principal telling me about one father who called and said, "I don't want my kid in that nigger lover's classroom, but I want him to learn to read, so put him in there, anyway." Obviously he thought he could undo all the damage I did in the area of human relations, but he couldn't teach him to read, so he had to take the bitter with the sweet.

The film crew was to come into Riceville during the third week in October and, interestingly enough, the race riots in Waterloo began on that Friday. Waterloo was only seventy miles from Riceville and many of my students had friends or relatives there. Darald and I had lived there for several years after we were first married (In fact, the National Tea Food Store that he managed was one of the first ones to be picketed for not having any black employees in the late 50's. He'd had black employees but at the time he was picketed, they'd all gone off to other jobs or to college, and he hadn't yet replaced them. Anna Mae Weems, who was spokeswoman for the local chapter of the NAACP Youth Council, organized and led the demonstration and ultimately became a helpful, albeit not friendly, acquaintance and advisor as Darald worked with the black community in which the store was located.) The riots became a perfect hook in October of 1968 on which to hang the Blue-eyes, Brown-eyes exercise.

The three-man CBC crew filmed in my room for three days, then took the film to Toronto and edited those three days into a half-hour show, which was inserted into the middle of a program about Eskimos. At that time, according to the members of the film crew, Eskimos in Canada were being called, "Niggers in Parkas."

The morning after the film was shown in Canada I got a call from the people at the CBC insisting that I come there on the following Saturday for a live interview. It seems their switchboard had nearly blown a fuse as viewers across the country had called in demanding to know what in Hell was going on with those poor little kids in Riceville, Iowa.

I went to Toronto the following Friday – while my luggage went to New York – to do what I expected to be a one-on-one interview with someone who wanted to present a rational, logical discussion of the exercise and its implications. Forget that! I walked into the studio and there, in the middle of the room, was a kidney bean-shaped dais on the floor, surrounded by risers in a semi-circle, on which were seated about two-hundred Canadians. I said to the interviewer, as I pointed at the dais, "What's that?"

He replied, "That's where we're going to sit."

Pointing to the risers, I asked, "Who are they?"

His reply was, "Those are the people who are going to interview you."

"This looks like a setup," I said.

"It is," he said, and taking my arm said, "Let's go." And to the dais we went. He introduced me by telling the audience members that this was Jane Elliott and she had come here to explain what she had been doing with her students in the third-grade classroom in Riceville, Iowa. Did anyone have any questions? Immediately two hundred angry Canadians raised their hands and commenced to interrogate me as to just what I thought I was doing with those poor little white children and that eye-color

48

thing. The interview was scheduled to last for one hour. It went on for four!

One of the first questions was asked by a white female (White females, watch your mouths!) . She said, "Mrs. Elliott, don't you think you could do great psychological damage to a child by doing that exercise with them for a day?" When I replied that I was more concerned with the damage that is done to people with whom we do this exercise based on skin color every day, and I was sure that she must be incensed about that, too, she replied, "That's different. They're used to it, they can take it." Does she really believe that the victims get used to racism and sexism and ageism and ethnocentrism and homophobia? God's nightgown! This was like being in the teachers' lounge in the Riceville Community Elementary School.

About half way through this interview an older white female stood up in the middle of the group and said, "Mrs. Elliott, I came here to tell you how much I hate you, not a surprise to me at this point. I am Jewish. I was born and raised in Germany. We went to a Jewish school. Every morning when our Headmaster came in, we would bow and say, 'Good morning, Herr Headmaster.' One morning he came in with two SS troopers and one of the troopers said to us, 'In the future you decadent Jews will no longer bow and say, 'Good morning, Herr Headmaster.' You will salute and say, 'Heil, Hitler.'" She continued, "I watched those who valued their life more than their faith salute and say, 'Heil Hitler.' I watched those who valued their faith more than life itself, continue to bow and say, 'Good morning, Herr Headmaster.' They disappeared and we never saw them again, but we know where they ended up." Then, after taking a deep breath, she said, "Your students are very fortunate. They will never allow what happened in our society to happen in yours; they'll see it coming and put a stop to it." Then she said something which frightens me to this day. She said, "The atmosphere that you created for the blue-eyed children in your classroom that day reminded me of the atmosphere that the Nazis created for the Jews in Germany."

Black people who see the film, The Eye of the Storm, which was made in my classroom the following year, say to me when the film is over, "That's the way I live every day of my life in this country." In 'the land of the free and the home of the brave,' where we have 'liberty and justice for all'?

Most white people reading this will say at this point, "I don't see it that way." Of course you don't; you're white and for the most part your reality is very different from the reality in which people of other colors live every day. Your freedoms are quite different from those extended to Blacks, and if people like the supporters of the arguments of Arthur Jensen, William Shockley, and Charles Murray have their way, those freedoms will only increase. Those of you who agree with Charles Murray's claim that IQ points should determine one's value to, and position in, society should immediately get to a psychologist and have your IQ tested. After you get the results I suggest that you contact Mr. Murray and ask whether he considers your score sufficient to qualify for acceptance in the upper echelons of his society. Don't be surprised if he asks you what color your skin is before responding to your question.

THINK, my dears, what a slippery slope we are on with this kind of political pollution. Remember that, as we get older our mental acuity changes. Will we finally be required to take yearly MA (Mental Age) tests to determine whether our IQ score is high enough for the government to pay our SS (Social Security)? If you think this sounds like science fiction, talk to any Holocaust survivor. Then, when you've convinced yourself that the person you've been speaking to is just "acting like a victim," read the book, <u>The Nazi Doctors</u>, by Robert J. Lifton. After that, in order to understand why people like Donald Trump and the Right To Lifers, say the things they do about immigration reform, and a woman's right to choose to have an abortion, read the book <u>The Birth Dearth</u>, by Ben Wattenberg – but don't buy it, just get it from the library. We must no longer contribute to his estate. Even though his life has ended, his influence is still very much alive.

6 "The road less...difference."

Since the exercise took place in October that year I had seven months to observe its effects on my students. They were considerable. One of the mothers thanked me, at our nine-week conference, for the difference I had made in her son.

"What have you done to him?" she asked. "We're actually glad to see him when he gets off the bus now. He's even nice to his little sister."

Another mother told me that she wished I could put her husband through the exercise because, she said, "I can't stop him and I don't want our kids to talk and think the way he does."

One day the students came in angry and agitated from the playground, grumbling and mumbling about the behaviors of the other third-grade teacher who had been on recess duty.

"What's going on here?" I asked. "What are you all so upset about?"

"It's that Mrs. ____," they all complained. "When we do something, she doesn't do a thing about it, but when that other group does the same thing she really gets on them. She's discriminating against them and somebody ought to tell her so!" Were they right? Of course they were; it was an ongoing problem. It wasn't a coincidence that she was also the one who said she thought 'it was about time somebody shot that son-of-a-bitch' about Martin Luther King Jr.

At Christmas time, when we discussed Peace on Earth, one child, who had rigorously refused to cooperate with discriminating against the inferior students on the day during which he was on the top, said that the way to have peace on earth was to make all grown-ups go through Discrimination Day.

When the rest of the community found out that I'd done the exercise in my classroom again, the rowdy, tough, noisy high school boys, who rode the buses, commenced to tease, taunt and ridicule my students on the way to and from school with statements like:

"You're the kids who have that nigger-lover for a teacher. You must all be nigger-lovers in that class!" The first time this happened, one of my boys came charging into class like he was ten feet tall.

"Boy, Mrs. Elliott," he said, "Did I learn something on the bus this morning!"

"What did you learn?" I asked him.

His reply was, "We already know it's wrong to use the word 'nigger' and we know there's nothing wrong with being one, either. And they're in high school, and they don't even know that!" Did I do my students harm by teaching them that discrimination was wrong and so exposing them to the possibility of ridicule, and, perhaps, more than just verbal abuse by their schoolmates? Or, did I do them a favor by making them aware of what racism really looks like and how all-pervasive it is in our society? The high school boys who taunted them were the ones they had looked up to and admired until that day. That experience created a new image of those big, bold, boisterous boys in the minds of my students. It was not an image they any longer seemed eager to emulate.

Because I had taken a course in Orton Gillingham Phonics, and so had learned how to teach the dyslexic child, my principal assigned only 16 students – all moderately to severely disabled readers – to my classroom the following fall (at least that's the reason he said he assigned them to me. I had to wonder, however, if those were the only students whose parents would allow their children to be in my room. An awful thought to take through the year. Was I just paranoid? Would you have been?)

I had been contacted in the summer by William Peters, a producer for ABC News, about the possibility of filming the eye-color exercise in my classroom for a television documentary. My first thought was, "Oh, God, Here we go again!" My second thought was, "Are these people crazy? Aren't there more exciting news stories out there?" I sent him to see Stephen Banker of the CBC and the film he'd made in order to give him a chance to change his mind. That didn't work. I sent him to my principal and superintendent, thinking that they could get me off the hook. That didn't work. I agreed to work with him. Then I saw my class roll. What a quandary! What an internal dialogue!

Question: Would it be unethical to put these learning disabled kids through this exercise?

Answer: Did you ask yourself that question last year, or the year before, when you knew you had learning disabled students in your class? Do we as a society ask ourselves that question before we put children of all colors through this exercise, but based on skin color, every day?

Question: What makes you think it will work again? These kids have heard all about this thing from their parents and their peers. What makes you think they'll react as previous students have?

Answer: Doesn't the skin-color exercise still work, even though it's been used in this country for about four-hundred years?

Question: What is your rationale for doing this exercise with the third-graders?

Answer: To make them aware of the damage done to the victims and the perpetrators of discriminatory treatment so that in the future when they witness racist behaviors they will recognize what's happening and refuse to go along. They may even be motivated by their memory of this day to try to stop the behaviors.

Question: Aren't you stretching a bit, here? What makes you think that these kids will remember this beyond the time they're in your room?

Answer: The kids who were in it before remember. Their parents have told me so. And the parents who've talked to me about it have been pleased at what their kids learned.

Question: Is this really necessary? You know that the first reaction you heard about coming from the community after your first exercise was, "Why is she doing that in Riceville? We don't have any racism here. We don't have any niggers."

Answer: That's the answer, isn't it?

Questions: That isn't going to be good enough when the shit hits the fan. And you know it will. How are you going to justify it to the principal?

Answer: He already gave his permission. He knows what it's all about. He saw last year's film and thought it was tremendous.

Question: Didn't he tell the film crew last year that it was just a harmless little exercise and that it probably wouldn't have any lasting effects?

Answer: That was before he saw the film. He also knows about the increased academic performance that we observed after the exercise, in both groups. Maybe that's the reason he agreed to this film being made.

Question: What if that was a fluke? What if it was just your imagination? How can you prove that what you thought you saw was real?

Answer: I'll test the kids before, during, and after the exercise to see if there's a difference in their academic performance.

Question: Where will you get the tests? There aren't tests available for something like this.

Answer: I'll write my own. I write tests all the time. I'll write four different but comparable tests, give one two weeks before the exercise, one each day of the exercise and one two weeks after the exercise, and compare the results.

Question: That'll never stand up in court. They'll say you faked the answers.

Answer: I'll send these tests to myself in the mail and not open them until I need them to use them as evidence, if that ever happens.

Question: Aren't you paranoid?

Answer: Remember that someone has said that just because you're paranoid, it doesn't mean they aren't out to get you.

Question: Get serious. Why are you really doing this exercise over and over again? Don't you just like all the attention?

Answer: I'm getting less attention than I've ever had in my life. In the school building I've become 'the invisible man'. If it weren't for the custodial staff and a couple of upper elementary teachers I wouldn't converse with adults from 7:30 in the morning until 4:30 in the afternoon, Monday through Friday. And, in the community, I've found out how "Typhoid Mary" must have felt. Do I like it? No, but it doesn't bother me like it did at first. However, it's becoming sort of comical: It's reached the point where, when someone speaks to me, I turn and look behind me to see who it is they're talking to. And I've got to admit that I'm beginning to enjoy needling them and rubbing it in a bit.

Question: Why not just stop doing it and let people forget it?

Answer: Because this exercise makes a positive difference in the lives of the children who experience it. If I quit doing it just to get along with my peers, I will have proven that my principles aren't as important to me as their acceptance of me is. I swore after that business in Waterloo that I'd never sacrifice my principles in this area again I learned a lot from that momentary experience so many years ago. It stayed with me and made a difference in my life. Perhaps what these kids learn from this experience will do something of the same thing for them.

Question: You were an adult making a choice for yourself; these are kids and you are making a choice for them. Do you have that right?

Answer: Do I have the right, knowing how their lives could be changed by this experience, not to do the exercise? When my own children were babies, I knew that we ran the risk of some very unpleasant side effects if I insisted that they get DPT shots. Yet, I did insist on the shots because I knew that the diseases we were trying to protect them from were much more dangerous than the side effects from the shots. This exercise is much like one of those inoculations: I am going to infect them with racism for one day in the hope that that brief experience will inoculate them against racism in the future. We all give our offspring the shots even though the likelihood of their being exposed to one of those diseases in this country is very rare. However, the likelihood of their being exposed to racism in this country isn't very rare: It's a guarantee. This isn't a, "What if?" situation. This is a "Since this is the way it is…" situation.

Question: Could you justify this to the teachers union?

Answer: I shouldn't have to.

Question: Could you justify this to the parents?

Answer: Yes…and much easier than I can justify teaching their children that George Washington never told a lie, and that Abraham Lincoln started the Civil War only in order to free the slaves.

Question: Could you justify this to God?

Answer: I hope I get the opportunity – but not right away.

Question: Can you justify this to Darald, and Sarah and Brain and Mary and Mark?

Answer: Not right now…I can only hope that someday the kids will understand and forgive me. Right now, all I can do is remind them that my dad always said, "A fair thing's a pretty thing and a right wrongs no man." Where Darald is concerned, I can only say, "Remember the part of that oh-so-short wedding ceremony where you said "for better or worse"? And, 'til death us do part'? And "I do"? Well, Honey, we did, and we are, and now, we will, won't we? Won't we?

Question: Do you expect to make money off this film? Are you going to charge ABC News for filming this thing?

Answer: And get accused of exploiting children for profit? I think not! Besides, if I got paid for this, I'd have to split every check I got 17 ways. I'd have to hire an accountant just to keep the IRS off my back. Furthermore, what kind of lesson would that be for my third-graders? If we go through this exercise one day in our lives, we get paid for doing it. How much do Black children get paid for going through this exercise every day of their lives? They aren't even allowed to suggest that it's happening.

Question: Someone could make big bucks off this thing. How do you feel about that?

Answer: It's a crapshoot, and I have no money on the table. Someone is spending money to put this together. I'll be teaching. That's what I get paid for. How much would it cost me to hire a film crew to come in here and make a film, with these dyslexic kids, that puts a lie to all the negative things that their previous teachers have said about them? I'm going to spend from August until February telling these kids how great they are, and then in February, ABC News is going to send a film crew in here and make a film that proves that everything I've said about them is true. How many dollars do you suppose that's worth?

Question: How are you going to keep these kids from mugging the camera?

Answer: I'm going to ask Charlotte Button to do a yearlong camera unit with these kids. We'll use the cameras that the CBC sent us last year and we'll take pictures of one another all year long. By the time the film crew gets here the kids will be accustomed to being in front of the camera.

Question: Where will you get the money for film and film processing?

Answer: I'll say to Darald, "Remember the part of that oh-so-short wedding ceremony where you said "for better or worse" and …"

Question: What if you get fired? Is doing this exercise more important to you than keeping your job?

Answer: As Dad would say, "I'd rather pick shit with the chickens than do something that I know is wrong, just to get ahead." I know this is right.

Question: What if this is a mistake and goes nowhere? You'll still be despised among your neighbors and peers for what you've done. What will have been accomplished?

Answer: If this is a mistake, it will die a natural death. If it's as good as I think it is you won't be able to beat it to death with a stick. Either way, I'm going to be despised, so I might as well just take 'the road less traveled'. And truly, that has made all the difference.

7 The Cure For Ignorance

March 1996

And so I did the BE/BE exercise in front of ABC's cameras and that film has been, and is being, used in all kinds of classes all over the world. As a result of people seeing the film, I have been invited to do the exercise with people of all ages and have re-learned the things that I learned with that first group of third-graders. I agreed to write this chapter because I think it's important that people at least read some of the most important things that I've learned. So, here goes.

I've decided that prejudice isn't the problem; discrimination is the problem. I think people in power choose a group of people who are different from the majority group and use that difference to justify discriminating against the target group. When the members of the targeted group react negatively to the treatment they are receiving, we use their negative reaction to prove that we were right to treat them as we did in the first place.

Prejudice is an attitude and by itself has no power. It is only when we begin to treat people positively or negatively because of our prejudices that we have a problem. President Dwight D. Eisenhower said, in response to black demands that he do something about the racism in this country, "You cannot legislate love". He was right; you can't legislate feelings, but you can legislate behavior. We do it all the time. You may feel resentment toward that new stop sign they've erected on your street corner, but you'll obey it because of the consequences if you don't. You may not like having a Black man in the White House, but you'll stand when he comes into the room, and you will not leave until he leaves. It's the law. Laws are used to change behaviors every day. However, they are usually written to the advantage of the people in power.

Nathan Rustein said that prejudice is an emotional commitment to ignorance. He was right. And, of course, the remedy for ignorance is education. However, that ignorance is harmful only when we act upon it. Be as ignorant as you choose; your prejudice can't hurt me. Hate me if you must. But, by the gods of war, you had best not discriminate against me, just because of your ignorance. Your opinion of me, or of anyone else, is your problem. Don't make it a problem for me, or for anyone else, by treating people badly simply because you flat-out don't know any better.

The first day of that first exercise, as I watched how my brown-eyed students treated me and their blue-eye peers, I found out how I look to people of color and that experience has changed the way I see my world and the people in it. It hasn't made me happy: "A little leaning is a dangerous thing", but it has made me more aware. Robert Burns, the Scottish poet said, "If some great power the gift could give us to see ourselves as others see us." I get that prayer answered, every time I do the exercise and watch Browns become me. White folks, you don't want that; it will ruin your exaggerated image of your own perfection.

I've learned, while watching the shouters and spitters and exaggerators on television, how powerful the media is and how dangerous it is when it is in the wrong hands and is being used for the wrong reasons. The media, at the direction of people with unlimited financial resources, are willing accomplices in keeping the fear and these –isms alive, because after all, fear sells programs and programs sell products and Capitalists are Kings. That, in my opinion, is exactly what's happening. I'm watching the media gin up situations all over the world, in an attempt, it seems to me, to further line the pockets of the owners of the industrial-military complex. Keep the masses frightened while we send their sons and daughters to fight in yet another old white men's war. And of course, making war and finding soldiers to fight them is so much easier if you've shipped most of your manufacturing jobs overseas, and prepared young men to be warriors by encouraging them to spend hours playing video games in which killing is routine and the winner is the one who kills the best, the most and the fastest. Dehumanize young people with what once would have been seen as indecent programming and then, when they become what they've been exposed to, accuse them of being bullies and savages, and send them to war.

Before I did the BE/BE exercise, I thought that prejudice caused discrimination. It had never occurred to me that, by designating a group as being inferior on the basis of a physical characteristic over which they had no control, and treating them as if they were, indeed inferior, I could convince them and everyone witnessing this event, that I was right in my judgment. By discriminating against the out-group, I caused them to become angry, resentful, resistant, timid, frightened and unable to perform academically. I forced them to live down to my expectations of them and then, when they did, blamed their behaviors on them, instead of taking responsibility for what I had forced them to become. Within 15 minutes, that first day – and every time I've done that exercise since, with different age groups and in different states, cities and countries – I taught my in-group students to be prejudiced toward those who had the wrong colored eyes, and to be willing to abuse them for that reason and that reason alone, for

God's sake! Kids of all ages aren't prejudiced on the basis of eye color, until I teach them to be. And since I have the power during the exercise, participants go along to get along, both those with the 'right' eyes, and those with the 'wrong' eyes.

I had never fully understood, until doing the exercise, how easy it is to hold onto power, no matter how undeserving you are of having it. You can appeal to the desire of all of us to be part of the power structure, to be accepted by the majority, and to be seen at least as one of the power players and so enlist others in your attempt to control people and situations. I watched students in my third-grade classroom, who had been friends for years, go to the dark side, in order to guarantee that they would not be treated as the inferior group members were being treated. As a grown man in an exercise in Kansas City said, when I asked him why he didn't defend one of the blue-eyed females, "Well, I knew it couldn't last forever, and as long as you were doing it to her, you weren't doing it to me."

Damn!!! Describing this whole thing was so easy when I knew that only my four offspring were going to be reading my words. Now, knowing that others may be reading them I keep self-censoring everything I say. At this rate, I'll never get past the second paragraph. Well, to hell with all that noise, here goes, and if this doesn't make for interesting reading, so be it.

8 The ABC's of the Storm

Getting the school administrators' permission to have the students filmed during the exercise in 1970 wasn't difficult: Mr. Brandmill, the elementary principal, had seen the CBC film and found it fascinating, and Mr. Johnston, the school superintendent trusted Brandmill's judgment. The parents, too, (with the exception of one father who said, "I was in the army with those people and I know what they're like," referring, of course, to Blacks) were, if not eager, at least willing to sign waivers granting ABC permission to make a television documentary starring their children. Just reading those waivers was an educational experience for us. They, as I recall, gave ABC the right to use the footage done in our classroom how and when they chose to, and we signed off any rights to any financial compensation for that footage. We signed. I, because I wanted this experience for my students, and the parents signed because, I guess, they saw some real value in what we were doing. And all of us, I suppose, signed because we were naïve – and vastly flattered that someone wanted to put these kids and this exercise on prime time television.

You see, when the principal assigned these students to me, he said, "Now, Mrs. Elliott, these kids are probably never going to learn to read. I know you get upset if kids don't succeed in your room, but don't get upset about these kids. Just do as much as you can with them. They're all probably going to drop out later on, anyway." These words from an administrator I truly admired!!! I was shocked and challenged. If I've been with a child for nine months I don't want that child to drop out – unless I'm pregnant, of course, and then, I push them out!

I was determined to prove Mr. Brandmill wrong about this group, and when I walked into that classroom on the first morning of the school year and saw those sixteen fragile, frightened, intimidated little 8 and 9 year olds looking at me, I swore that they'd learn to read, come Hell or high water, and we'd prove that their previous teachers and the principal were grossly mistaken in their assessments of these kids and their abilities.

It wasn't an easy task. Some of these 16 students had been through kindergarten, junior first grade, first grade and second grade and had experienced virtually no success in those four years. Two of them had been identified as being mentally retarded by the professionals who had tested them during their previous school years. Their eyes were dull and some of them were as wary as wild fawns, not trusting me but wishing they could. One of them was a serious stutterer; one had a severe speech problem, almost speaking a language all her own. Several came from what educators like to refer to as "disadvantaged homes", but which I recognized as being supportive and rich in care, if not in material things. Most of them had been described to me by their previous teachers as being either low IQ, lazy or behavior problems.

I realized from those descriptions and from my experience with some of their older siblings that these kids were probably dyslexic and would have difficulty with visual learning. So the first thing I did was teach them the listening skills, which I had learned from Dr. James Daugherty of Drake University. What Dr. Daugherty said, I believed, and his listening skills have made all the difference in the world for me as a student and as a teacher. Those listening skills are as follows:

1) Good listeners have quiet hands, feet and mouths.
2) Good listeners keep their eyes on the person who is speaking.
3) Good listeners listen from the beginning to the very end.
4) Good listeners decide to learn something.

I told the kids that I expected them to learn these skills and to practice them. They were practically the only rules we would need in our classroom. Then I introduced them to the point system. This was a behavior modification system which I had learned from my critique teacher, Mrs. Hazel Grant, in Independence, Iowa, as I did my student teaching under her supervision.

I had arranged the desks in four rows of four. Now I appointed row leaders for each of the rows based on the alphabetical order of the names of the students in each row, and checked points. If every child in a row had a clean desk, a handkerchief or tissue, and a sharpened pencil, the row got three tally points on the chart on the chalkboard. It being the first day of school, every child had all these items – or did after I passed around the Kleenex box off my desk – so every row got three points plus a bonus point for having everything! Success#1! Then I told them that a row could earn points by being the first row ready for recess, or lunch, or working. They could also earn points by being helpful to others and by being good listeners! However, if they didn't practice the listening skills or if they ran in the halls, they'd have to take off a point. At the end of the week, the row with the most points would get into the grab-bag. The grab-bag was a brown paper grocery bag which held novelty erasers, small tablets, colored pencils, pencil sharpeners, and small packs of Kleenex; the things that third graders at that time found exciting as well as useful. Their eyes lit up at the sight of the grab-bag—much as the teachers' eyes lit up when they discussed their salary increases every year.

After counting points and stressing the importance of practicing the listening skills, I began the learning for the day. On this day and every day of the year, I started by reading poems to them and challenging them to repeat the end rhymes of the lines after me. You see, words had been tools of torture for these kids for three or four years and I had to bring to them a love of the language, if they were ever to learn to read, write or speak it with any degree of confidence. How better to bring them that love than with things like, "The People" and "Firefly" by Elizabeth Madox Roberts, Carl Sandburg's "Splinter" and "Slippery", "Little Brother's Secret" by Katherine Mansfield, "Grizzly Bear" by Mary Austin, "Little Orphant Annie" by James Whitcomb Riley, "Windy Nights" by Robert Louis Stevenson, "The Falling Star" by Sara Teasdale, "The Last Word of a Bluebird" by Robert Frost, "Easter" by Joyce Kilmer, "Wisdom" and "April Rain Song" by Langston Hughes, and anything (almost) written by Shelly Silverstein (You have to be kind of careful with some of his poetry.) We "did poetry" and the kids thought they were getting out of work every time there was a lull in the day's activities, all year. By the end of the year, they could recite between fifty and a hundred poems—including all of "Little Orphant Annie". When I'd ask, "Who knows a poem?" at various times during the day that year thirty-two hands would shoot up…they all knew several poems and were thrilled to say them.

After the poetry session we got down to the "real business" of learning. I assigned review seat work for them to do independently, while I informally tested them individually, to determine their reading level and to find out whether the mistakes they made were those characteristic of the dyslexic child. Their reading levels were mostly in the first and lower second grade levels and the mistakes they made when reading the word lists were mostly those I'd seen in my previous dyslexic students. It didn't take long to test only sixteen students so, by noon, I was prepared to sit down with them and explain to them what they and I could expect during the coming year.

"Look, kids," I said. "Here's the way I see it. I see 16 really bright, sharp, eager, cooperative kids who want to learn to read but have had a hard time doing it. I also see some kids who've been called 'dumb' and 'slow' and 'stupid' by someone. Is that what's been happening?" Most of them nodded or looked away, not wanting to meet my eyes.

'Well," I said, "I don't see any dumb or stupid or slow kids here. I see here the kids I'd most want to teach if I could have my pick of all the kids in the third grade this year. I also see 16 students who have a specific reason for having trouble learning to read and I know what that reason is." I then wrote the word 'on' on the board and asked them what it was. Some of them said, "on," some said, "no," some said nothing. I then did the same thing with the word 'was'. Some said, "was," some said, "saw," some said nothing. I then explained to them that some people don't always see the words the way they're written or hear words the way they're said and so, in order to learn to read and spell, we need to be taught in a special way and, I said, "I know that way!" I went on (I do tend to go on, don't I?), "If you do what I tell you to, I am willing to guarantee that you'll be able to read when you leave this classroom at the end of the year. Do you believe that?" They looked at one another with the "Do we dare believe it" look in their eyes. I laughed and said, "Wait, just you wait. You'll see. Let's go to work."

I split the class according to the reading levels at which they'd performed on the informal testing that morning, and we went to work learning how to read using the Orton/Gillingham Phonics materials and methods. By the end of that reading period, every child in the group had been successful at spelling and reading at least 20 words, many of which they'd never been able to read or spell consistently before. Successes #'s 2-20!!

Am I a miracle worker? No! Do I have a secret, or some special skill? No! I simply used what I had learned in a course in Orton/Gillingham Phonics at the Reading Center in Rochester, MN. The Center was run by, and the teaching was done by, two remarkable women, Paula Rome and Jean Osman, and the course is still being offered to anyone who wants practically every child in his/her classroom to learn to read.

That first day of school was the beginning of 6 months of building trust in me into my students; confidence in their own abilities into the students; confidence in my ability to teach them what they needed to know, and interest and excitement into the classroom.

In September we studied insects in science (and every other area of the curriculum); this meant sewing insect nets out of old pillowcases (good eye/hand coordination, small motor skills development, following directions); catching, killing (humanely), identifying and classifying insects (vocabulary development, categorizing, visual discrimination training, etc., etc.); learning "buggy" poems, and writing our really buggy poetry. We did everything but eat insects and, if I'd been able to find some chocolate covered ants, we would've done that. As it was, we had to settle for studying bees and eating honey.

In social studies we learned about foods, which meant that we, among many other things, churned butter by shaking cream in a jar; visited a real creamery (their churn was bigger than ours but their butter was no better); visited an egg processing plant; sampled numerous foods they'd never eaten before (third graders are not thrilled by caviar); and learned about the origins of many foods. As a culminating activity we made our own lunch in the classroom one day. The entrée was hamburger soup. Try it, you'll like it. My kids did.

Recipe for Hamburger Soup:

3 T. butter, melted   *4 carrots, pared, sliced ¼ inch thick*
1-1/2 lb. ground beef   *¼ cup chopped celery tops*
1 onion   *`¼ cup chopped parsley*
1 can (1 lb.12oz) tomatoes, undrained   1 bay leaf
3 cans (10-1/2 oz) condensed beef consume, undiluted
½ tsp. Italian seasoning
10 whole black peppercorns   *½ tsp. thyme*

Melt butter in large kettle. Add onions and soften. Add beef, cook, stirring over medium heat, 5 minutes or until meat loses its angry red look. Add remaining ingredients, along with 2 cups water; bring to boiling. Reduce heat; simmer, covered, 45 minutes, stirring occasionally.

In November we learned about clothing, where it came from, and how it is made. As a culminating activity for that unit we opened our own Room 10 Clothing Store. Each child brought in used clothing which was in good shape but no longer fit him/her. The Room 10 Store purchased the items from the students, paying for them in special Room 10 money; marked each item up by one-third, and then displayed each item on the shelves, tables or racks which we had improvised from various materials in the room. After a week of collecting our store's "inventory" we had a grand opening and each child used his/her Room 10 money to purchase items brought in by their classmates. Those who had been unable to bring merchandise to the store were hired to run the cash registers and restock the shelves, so every child had money to spend in the store at some time. Most of the students did their Christmas shopping for their younger siblings in the Room 10 Store. I took numerous outgrown items from my own offsprings' closets to the store and watched those clothes be worn, and subsequently sold, in Room 10 in the following years.

One year, we decided we should open a bank and deposit our money in it so that everyone could just write checks instead of carrying around all those little pieces of money. That worked well until one boy wrote a check for more money than he had in his account. The "clerk" at the bank announced that we'd better open a jail because Richard had written a bad check. At that point Richard said, "I've got some more in my desk! Wait! Wait!" He made a mad dash for his desk, rummaged about in it, and then came dashing back to deposit his funds and, shaking his head in relief, said, "Now I know what my dad means when he says he's gotta' beat a check to the bank!"

One of the boys in the '69 school year spotted a white shirt in our store that would just fit him. Since he had a wedding to attend in the coming summer and no shirt to wear, he asked if he could put this shirt on layaway until he got enough money to pay for it. We agreed that that would be alright and then, he commenced to come up to me and say, "Here's ten cents. Now how much do I need for that shirt?"

"Go to the board and figure it out," I said. So he did. This happened several times before I realized what was going on. I knew that he was one of the store's employees, since he hadn't been able to bring in any merchandise and we hadn't had a payday yet, so I asked, "Are you borrowing money from your friends?"

"Yeah," he answered, "They have lots of it! They don't care."

I said, "Wait a minute! You have to sign an IOU for each amount you borrow and you have to pay that money back." Okay, no problem. He papered the room with IOUs, paid for the shirt, and took it home in total joy! On the very next day, his oh-so-generous friends started calling in those IOUs. He was frantic; he had no clothes to sell and had to start selling off his "treasures". We, of course, paid him more for his items than they were worth and he finally came up to my desk after several days and said, "Well, I got all my money paid back, but I'm not happy."

"But Greg," I said, "think how good you'll look in that shirt this summer. Won't you be happy then?"

"Yeah," he grumped, "but that doesn't help me now."

"Well, have you learned anything" I asked.

"Yeah," he said, "I'm never going to borrow another dime as long as I live!"

On the closing day of the Room 10 Store that year, we had an auction to get rid of our leftover stock. I was the auctioneer and at one point Sandy and another student were furiously bidding against one another on an item of clothing. The other girl had stopped bidding but Sandy kept right on yelling out larger and larger bids. "Sandy!" the others laughed, "you're bidding against yourself!!"

Sandy would have suffered great embarrassment but for Roy Wilson who reached out to her and said, "That's okay. Sandy's excited. She's never been to a real live auction before." I guess you know he got to put up points for that kindness.

Several years later three of my former students and I were in the local barber shop waiting to get our hair cut. We began to visit about some of the things that we remembered from their time in Room 10. One of those junior high students said, "My little nephew is wearing those little red rubber overshoes that I bought in the Room 10 Store." My own sons and daughters had outgrown those boots before I sold them to the Room 10ers.

After the boys left, and I was in the chair, the barber said to me, "I've never heard kids talk that way before. They remember everything you did!"

For the rest of that year little girls would come to school wearing their classmates' clothing and the garment's previous owner would say,

"That blouse looks better on you than it did on me." The store created cousins out of friends and it was remarkable!

The kids took lots of pictures of one another that year. I had a friend, Charlotte Button, who was a professional photographer and, since we knew that the television crews were coming in February, we wanted to get the kids used to being in front of the camera. We took pictures of them during the first couple weeks of school so that we could have before pictures to compare with the after pictures that we planned to take at the end of the year. By the end of January those kids were lookin' and feelin' and doin' good!

Then came February and National Brotherhood Week and Bill Peters and the ABC "Now" show's crews. I told my students that the film crew was coming and when they asked why they were coming to our classroom, I said, "Because they're looking for the greatest group of third graders they can find, and where would they go except to my room?"

"Okay, Mrs. Elliott, if you say so," they responded. After all, I'd been telling them since the first day of the school year what great people and marvelous students they were, and here was the ultimate proof that I hadn't been lying!

I walked into my classroom that Monday morning to find that

it had been turned into a mini soundstage: the drapes were drawn across the windows, the area in front of the windows was an organized mess of cameras and sound equipment, the overhead lights had been supplemented by lights attached to boards attached to the overhead lights and there were, it seemed to me, big people carrying microphones, cameras, clapboards, and equipment all over the place. My students were enthralled, once they had been introduced to the members of the crew and they overcame their initial shyness. The camera crew, headed by Vince Gaito and the sound crew, headed by Morgan Smith, demonstrated the working and the use of the equipment to them, and to a number of other classes whose teachers brought them to the room during the day. By the end of the day, the kids were accustomed to the presence of the strangers among us and were able to proceed with business as usual. This may have been partially the result of my having told them during the previous week that if they played "Look At Me" during the filming, the crew would pack-up their equipment and leave.

"Look At Me" was the name we used for behaviors designed to get undeserved attention. It's what fathers – and, sometimes, mothers – do when they stand on the sidelines during an athletic event and shout insults and obscenities at the coach for his decisions. It's what hecklers do during the comedian's act in a lounge. It's what audience members do, when they stand and ask questions that have already been answered by the speaker, during a lecture or presentation. It's part of what motivates many people to volunteer to appear on daytime talk shows. It's often counterproductive and, in the classroom, it wastes a lot of time. It's seeking recognition without having done anything remarkable, and my students and I had little time for it.

Perhaps my students' awareness of, and aversion to, "Look At Me" was part of the reason for the very real emotions they displayed and the verbal responses they made to the "Blue-eyes/Brown-eyes" exercise during the rest of that week. These students' reactions were very similar to the reactions of my previous students and are amply described in Bill Peters' book, <u>A Class Divided, Then and Now</u>, and depicted in the film, <u>The Eye of the Storm.</u>

However, some of the unique events of that week were not included in the film. One of the members of ABC's group had just come back from covering the famine which was occurring in Biafra. I asked him what disturbed him the most about what he had experienced there and he replied, "I haven't been able to get a decent hamburger in two weeks." He and I didn't communicate well after that.

Russell Ring swallowed a straight pin on Tuesday and had to be rushed to the hospital in Osage, 17 miles away, since there was the danger of the pin becoming lodged in his digestive tract. Fortunately, he passed the pin the following day, but when the nurse presented him with the pin, as they prepared to release him from the hospital, he said, "That's not my pin. My pin was nice and shiny." No one had told him about the effect of the stomach acids on the pin's metal.

Sheila Shaefer ran into the steel upright on the swing set on the playground and got a goose egg the size of my thumb on her forehead. It looked fearsome and was obviously painful. Would it have happened if she hadn't been thinking about what was going on in the classroom and in her head? I don't know.

One of my colleagues accosted a member of the film crew in the hall and said, "Why are you concentrating on Elliott's classroom? There are interesting things going on in our rooms, too."

On Thursday, members of my previous two years' classes were interviewed by the film's narrator, Bill Beutel, and when I walked by the windows of the library where the interviews were being held, Vince Gaito put his face close to the window of the library and mouthed to me, "They hate you!" I was crushed! I went back to my room in near tears, deeply regretting three years of work and those four days of filming.

They took that four days of filming to New York and edited it down to a half hour show which was telecast in the early part of May. I had thought the local reaction to the Carson show was unpleasant. That was only a dress rehearsal for what happened after The Eye of the Storm, as the show was titled, was telecast.

John Leonard in a Life magazine review described the show as "a quiet and effective television half hour" while Max Rafferty in various newspapers called it "educational malfeasance."

Parents whose children weren't in my classroom called it a disgrace and grounds for my dismissal, while some of the parents whose children were in the exercise called it the best thing that had ever happened to their children in a classroom. I heard their comments secondhand, for the most part, because no one in the community said much to me. About anything!!! My offspring and my parents weren't so fortunate. My parents operated a hotel with a small restaurant in it in Riceville. On the day before "The Eye of the Storm" was shown on television, they sold numerous breakfasts, lots of coffee and forty-five lunches in their restaurant. Riceville is a tiny town so these numbers weren't bad. On the day after "Eye..." was shown they sold two lunches. The customers stayed away in droves after that. My parents finally simply closed the dining room. It didn't destroy them financially, since they owned a 160-acre farm which had been in my father's family for nearly a hundred years, but it did shake their belief in the goodness of some of the Christians who had been their friends, neighbors, and customers for years.

When Vinni Gaito said to my mother, "She's got a bear by the tail", in describing his reaction to what he'd seen happen in my classroom, I didn't realize that the townspeople were included in his prediction. I was honestly naïve enough to think (believe? hope?) that once the people in the community realized how great the learning had been and how important the concepts were, they'd be proud and impressed with what was happening in this little rural community, rather than being angry and threatened. Wrong, again!

Our family learned a great deal from the reactions to the exercise: That fall when Brian, our oldest son, went to junior high, he was a constant target for the students, some of the teachers and coaches, and the junior high principal. Even the bus driver, who drove the physical education bus from the elementary building to the junior high, consistently managed to close the doors of the bus just before Brian got on and, laughing, pull away as Brian ran after the bus. He had to run, because if he came into the building later than his peers, he was in real trouble with the principal.

I came home from school one day to find Brian, bruised and bloody, beaten and bashed. "What in God's name happened to you?" I asked. Seems he'd been being chased home from school for a couple of weeks by several high school guys in their car. Since the junior high school students were released earlier than the high schoolers were and the junior high building was closer to home than the high school was, he had always been able to get home safely. On this day, he hadn't hurried fast enough and a carload of five high school kids caught up with him. Three brave boys jumped out and beat him up while the other two stayed in the car, one to drive and other to serve as watchman to avoid their getting caught. Over Brian's protest I called the kid's parents. None seemed shocked; one indicated that Brian had gotten what I deserved! One boy's mother was one of my fellow teachers and she sent him over to apologize. When I called the principal about what was happening to Brian, his response was, "I don't care who you are or what you've done. I've got your kid up here now and I'm going to take care of him."

I'd have thought that the things that were happening to Brian were his fault if they hadn't also been Sarah's lot when she was in the junior high. When I asked one of her teachers at conference, a year earlier, what she could do about the ugly things that were being said and done to Sarah, she replied, "I knew this was going to happen. You should have thought of this before you did that eye thing."

I might still have thought it was just my paranoia if Mrs. Brandmill, who taught home economics at the junior high, hadn't confirmed my suspicions. She said to me, "Get your kids out of this school, Jane. These teachers are trying to destroy your children."

As I read back over what I've written and relive the rage I felt when Brian and Sarah were being abused by their peers, I try to tell myself that the abusers were acting out of ignorance and fear, and that I should forgive them. Then I remember one of the things Elie Weizel said when he spoke at Luther College in Decorah, Iowa. He said, "The Jews say you have the right to forgive others for what they do to you; you do not have the right to forgive them for what they do to others. Only those others have that right."

I also remember how often my dad said, "It's a long road that has no turning." He also said, "Time heals all wounds," but Brian and Sarah still hope that time wounds all heels. I'm with them.

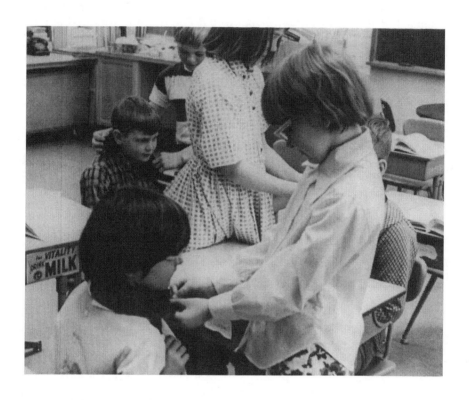

Brown-eyed students pin collars on Blue-eyed students.
Charlotte Button 1970

Students lined up to go to lunch.
Charlotte Button 1970

Jane, students, and members of the film crew in the classroom.
Charlotte Button 1970

Students joyously remove collars.
Charlotte Button 1970

Jane and students, all together again, happy the exercise is over.
Charlotte Button 1970

9 Children Without Prejudice in D. C.

In December of that year I was invited to be a forum member for the White House Conference on Children and Youth in Washington, D.C. Those conferences used to be held every 10 years, but Ronald Reagan, while President, decided that the conference was a waste of public funds—he probably made that decision during the same week that he decided that ketchup was a vegetable—so, the conferences are no longer being held.

I asked the person who called me why they'd decided to invite me to this conference and he replied, "We've looked high and low and you're the only classroom teacher we've been able to find who's doing anything meaningful in the area of reducing prejudice in children." Now that's depressing. But I wasn't depressed; I was flattered and delighted. I immediately called Mr. Johnston, the superintendent, and asked for a week of professional leave to attend the White House Conference on Children and Youth in Washington, D.C. His response to my request was,
"What 'house' conference?"

I replied, "The White House Conference."

"Oh, that house…" he said. Then, "Yes, I guess that'll be alright." So, during the second week in December, I flew to D.C. to meet with the other forum members and to decide what our forum, which was entitled "Children Without Prejudice", was going to present as a special experience for our forum delegates. We had already been mau-maued by a group of angry Blacks during a fact-finding trip to San Antonio, TX, and severely dressed down by Piri Thomas, the Puerto Rican author of <u>Down These Mean Streets,</u> for plans we'd discussed during a pre-conference planning session in D.C., so it was not a shock to me when, at Pat Okura's suggestion, the forum members asked me to conduct the Blue-Eyes/Brown-Eyes exercise with our 180+ forum delegates. Since fools rush in where angels fear to tread, I agreed to do as they asked.

On the day of the exercise we split the delegates according to eye color as they came up to the door of the meeting room. The Browns were sent into the meeting room while the Blues were told to wait over against the opposite wall in the hall until we needed them. This separating was done by Manuel Ortiz, a large Hispanic elementary school principal from San Antonio, Texas, and Piri Thomas, who acted the part of an angry, embittered security guard to perfection. His, "Get over there with the rest of those Blueys," and, "You Blueys hold it down. We don't wanta' hear your noise," did exactly what we wanted to have done to the group. We took the Browns into the meeting room and told them what we were going to do. At this point, one liberal white female indicated that she didn't think this was fair and she didn't want to participate. Pat Okura stood to respond to her statement. (Pat Okura, a child psychologist, was a Japanese American who was relocated from his home in California during the Second World War. He was sent to the Santa Anita racetrack for several weeks and then to a detention camp in the California desert where he was to spend the duration of the war. Shortly after his arrival at the detention camp, Father Flanagan of Boys Town contacted the administrators of the camp and requested that they allow several of the detainees to come and work at Boys Town. He needed, among other experts, a child psychologist. Pat Okura spent the remainder of the war years and ten years after that at Boys Town.) He quickly explained to our Timid Tillie why she needed to participate in this exercise and how fortunate she was that she had a choice as to whether to be a party to unfairness, since many of us are forced to participate in unfair situations every day and know that the consequences will be dire if we choose not to go along. Her enthusiasm for protest was effectively and immediately squelched.

Now, you must bear in mind that the delegates to the WHCCY were educated, intelligent, expert individuals who were instrumental in improving the lives of children throughout the U.S. There were doctors and lawyers, teachers and preachers, psychologists and psychiatrists, politicians and social workers, and welfare recipients and wealthy philanthropists. All considered themselves mature, worthwhile adults who had come to D.C. to give the President of the United States the benefit of their knowledge and expertise.

After some time and much discussion with the Browns we finally let the Blueys into the room, but insisted that they remain on the chairs in the area at the back of the room. They'd been standing in the hall outside for over half an hour and were looking forward to sitting down, so it was not a joyful moment when they discovered that we'd only provided enough chairs for half of them. At this point they tried to present a list of demands which they'd compiled out in the hall. We ridiculed them, of course, and refused to read their demands. They immediately became hostile. No surprise; everyone knows Blueys are easily aroused to anger. After all, it's genetic. Pat Okura stepped forward once again and announced that the Blueys must give up their plastic zippered packets which the conference organizers had given each of the delegates. "After all," as he reminded us, "you never know what kinds of weapons Blueys might be carrying." The Blueys set up a howl of protest, refusing to comply with his request. Those who were on chairs promptly put their packets on their chair seats and sat on them.

Unfazed, Okura said, with a totally straight face, "Okay. Let them keep them, now that they're sitting on them: that's the only part of their anatomy that can absorb knowledge anyway." I commenced to describe Blueys and their belligerent behaviors as we had already observed them and to announce the rules for the day, whereupon a large, blond female began to lead her blue-eyed peers in singing, "We Shall Overcome." I found this extremely distasteful since it was so obviously an attempt to "play black," so the Browns drowned out her feeble attempt at protest by singing "Beautiful Brown Eyes."

Now the Blondie from Boston shouted, "Let's caucus! All you Blue-Eyes gather round and we'll caucus!" Now Browns began to sing "God Bless America" as sanctimoniously and sincerely as it's ever been sung. This so enraged Blondie that she decided to lead 'her people' in a demonstration, so, she forced her way to the front of the room where she and a large group of the Blues sat down on the floor. Absolutely the worst move she could have made, for in doing so she proved that everything we had said about them was true; they were aggressive, belligerent, anti-social, ignorant, uncivilized and unclean (they had already littered the entire area around them and had torn some of the one-of-a-kind photos off the walls and thrown them on the floor). Each statement they uttered and each behavior they exhibited was further proof that we had not stereotyped them unfairly.

While this was going on, I noticed a young black male who had come into the room late. He stood in the back of the room for a short time, listening to what was being said and done and then came charging down the center aisle shouting,

"Stop this! What are you people doing? We came here to talk about children without prejudice and look at what you grownups are doing!"

I stepped in front of him before he got to the front of the room and sharply asked, "What color are your eyes?"

"I don't know!" he cried in frustration. "What difference does it make?"

"Well, they must be blue or you'd at least know what color they are," I snapped. "Now go to the back of the room where you belong and stay there!" In confusion and anger he threw his hands into the air and turned and fled to the back of the room, complaining and looking for comfort and support. One of the blue-eyed forum members quickly took him by the arm and led him aside to try and explain what was happening in the room. He was inconsolable. The Blueys who had no chairs and who refused to sit on the floor had been milling about in the aisle and in the rear of the room trying to strategize. An older brown eyed female, seeing the discomfort of a young blue-eyed woman standing beside her chair, stood and offered her chair to the Bluey.

Immediately Blondie from Boston yelled out, "Look at that! She gave her chair to a blue-eye! See? Not all Brown-eyes feel the way you do!"

"Yes," I said, "that older brown-eyed woman was kind enough to offer that Bluey a chair and she, even though she's much the younger of the two, took it and is letting that older female stand. What does that tell you about blue-eyed people?" At this, both women became extremely uncomfortable, the one on the chair because she was being made to look rude and inconsiderate, and the one who'd given up her chair because her good deed was resulting in exactly the opposite of what she'd intended, which was to give comfort to another human being.

By now it was past time to break for lunch and Pat Okura announced that we were going to adjourn for the morning but that no Blueys were to leave the room, because they might vandalize other areas of the building if they were allowed to wander at will. At that, Blondie and her fellow Blueys leapt from the floor and the chairs and charged for the door.

"Don't let them out," Okura called to Ortiz and Thomas, but of course his calls were to no avail. The Blueys literally slammed the two men out of their way, crashed through the doors, and dashed out into the hall, looking for someone in authority to whom they could complain about the way they'd been treated. We forum members were immediately surrounded by security guards and ushered away to lunch. They had been sent to the room to quell the riot which someone had reported taking place in the Children Without Prejudice forum.

In the afternoon the Blueys refused to come back into the room in which they had been so mistreated, so the conference organizers had to find "neutral ground" for the afternoon session.

The discussion of the morning's events was frank and open and I believe, honest. At one point a white, blue-eyed female leaned forward in her seat and said, "I feel that I have to tell you what I went through this morning. I knew you were wrong and I knew, intellectually, that I should try to do something to stop you, but something inside me said to me, 'They're just going to do it to you anyway, so you might as well just sit here and take it'. And that," she said, "is exactly what I did. I just sat here and took it."

By this time she and numerous other people in the room were in tears. And why not? Did we learn anything? I did. I learned, again, that when you treat people unfairly on the basis of a physical characteristic over which they have no control, regardless of their age or gender or profession or educational level or status in the community, they will react negatively, sometimes verbally and sometimes physically to the treatment. No one, it seems to me, is immune to the pain and frustration that results from being treated unjustly. I also learned, again, that some people will collude with evil if, by so doing, they can prevent the perpetrators from targeting them. In addition, I learned that intelligent people who exhibit rational behaviors could be seen and judged as irrational by the powerful people in an irrational society.

**<u>Washington Star</u> article,
Wednesday, December 16, 1970, pg. C-7:**

'BLUE EYES GET PICKED ON'
Lesson in Prejudice, by Toni House, Star Staff Writer
A heavy-set, sever-looking man stopped me at the door of the Forum 18 meeting room. "You have blue eyes," he said, blocking my way and handing me a black armband. "Put this on and wait outside."

And that is how about one-third of the 100-plus forum members and I were introduced to the fact that we were about to take a journey as an instant and abhorred minority group, Blue-eyed people.

It was compelling, frightening and sometimes musing journey into discrimination for us Blue-eyes (and green and hazel eyes, too). It was a quick lesson in second-class citizenship for people who personally have suffered only from the relatively petty (we learned) annoyances of our society.

Nerves

Our reactions began almost immediately. We huddled together in the dim hall of the Sheraton Park. It took us only a few minutes to psyche out the reason for our exclusion – we were about to become the victims of Jane Elliott, an Iowa school teacher who made headlines in 1968 when she first led her third graders in "discrimination day" exercises.

But the knowledge that it was only a game we were about to play did little to alleviate our mounting nervousness as we shifted uncomfortably under a barrage of standard, but to us new, abuse from the doorkeeper.

"You, you Blue-eyed People – always late," he'd scolded, or "Can't you see you're blocking the way of this Brown-eyed Person. It's a good thing I'm a Christian."

When we were allowed in, it took just a few minutes of "back of the room" insults for group personalities to begin to form. Three "militants" rushed Mrs. Elliott for front row seats.

At confrontation, one girl gasped, "But You have blue eyes!"

Mrs. Elliott was not shaken by the revelation. "I'm married to a brown-eyed man," she retorted.

"We hope YOU people can behave yourselves... YOU people will have to be quiet...YOU people get us some more chairs...insults heaped on insults...blue – brown tension grew.

We braced for violence as the "superiors' tried to take our conference packets for fear they contained knives (Blue-eyed People can't shoot straight") but we sat on them.

Sinking In

It began to seem the "game" would never end. We tried reason. Some Blue-eyes sank in the chairs in abject submission. We wanted out. A large blonde from Boston rose to lead us to the door. The doorkeeper blocked out was and we submitted to captivity.

We staged a front-of-the-room sit-in.

Suddenly, a sweet-faced, Brown-eyed, young man burst down the aisle quivering with rage. "Stop it! Stop it!" he demanded passionately of Mrs. Elliott. "We're here to talk about discrimination and prejudice...There's been two much already...and you all are talking about EYES!" He was not kidding, he had come in late and thought it was for real.

By the time we broke for a Blue-eyed caucus, we had all settled in [our] relative roles of radicalism. Some were for picketing: some for tearing up the meeting room; some for reason and love. We even had an Uncle Tom: "But Brown-eyed People have always been nice to me."

When we returned, the game was over. We laughed with the Brown-eyes and sat where we pleased. Small rap groups sprung up as we swapped experiences and emotions. Although the excitement still was high, we Blue-eyes had begun to relax.

Dissenters

It was, after all, still a game. At the end of an hour, we had gotten out.

Not everyone was delighted with the "exercise," as its tiny originator, Jane Elliott, of Riceville, Iowa, insisted on calling it.

Dr, Bruce Lee adamantly termed it a waste of conference time, although numerous Blue-eyes tried to tell him they had learned form it. "You white women go play your game. You can jump in and out. Black children can't," he said.

Mrs. Elliott said she felt the exercise important to adults. First, it was a personal experience, she said, second, a demonstration of teaching technique.

After a week of being in the (for me) rarefied atmosphere of D.C., and being in the company of people who expressed a commitment to do something positive to change the level of racism in the children in this society, I returned to Riceville to find my own fourteen year old daughter, Sarah, confused and distant. When she and I finally got a chance to visit about what was bothering her, she said, "Mom, Ann (her very best friend) told me that you must be planning on having intercourse with somebody in

Washington, DC. Did you?"

I was stunned and said, "Of course I wasn't Sarah. My God, whatever gave her that idea?"

Sarah said, "Well, you took that douche bag along and Ann says the only reason a woman has for using that is to keep from getting pregnant."

I laughed heartily at that and said, not very kindly, I know, "No wonder Ann has eight or nine siblings, if that's what her mother is using for birth control. No, Sarah, I have a yeast infection and the doctor prescribed regular douches as part of the remedy." Sarah learned about ignorance and friendship and feminine hygiene.

I brought Sarah a rather nice little denim purse from DC, which she proudly carried to school. She came home from school several days after school resumed in January in angry tears. She had left her purse on the shelf under the mirror in the girls' restroom while she went into one of the stalls. When she came out she found that the handles had been cut off the purse and her lipstick been used to write words "nigger lover" on the mirror above it. When she showed it to the principal he said he didn't know that somebody else did it: Perhaps she did it herself to get attention. Sarah learned about ignorance and cowardice and professional ethics.

That Easter our friends, Dr. Shirley Pearl and her husband, Harold, were guests in our home for the weekend. Now, Shirley is an unnatural blond and Harold is a natural black. Very. When we returned to school on the following Monday, Mary's little sixth grade classmates formed a circle around her in the hall and, in the presence of their white male teacher, one of them loudly pronounced,

"My dad said he wondered how long it would be before your mom was sleepin' with those nigger men." The teacher did nothing. Mary learned about ignorance and collusion and professional ethics.

10 The Proof is in The Pudding

After I'd done the exercise yearly for four or five years, an associate professor from the Teachers College of Iowa in Cedar Falls (now renamed the University of Northern Iowa), approached Superintendent Johnston and me and requested our approval for conducting an attitudinal survey of the third, fourth, fifth and sixth graders in the Riceville Community School. The purpose of the survey was to measure the level of racism in those students' attitudes. Mr. Johnston and I readily agreed to the survey, particularly after the professor told us that he was going to conduct the same survey in the school in Saint Ansgar, a nearby comparable community.

A few weeks after he'd conducted the survey he returned to Riceville to tell us that, upon tabulating the results, he'd discovered that the Riceville students who had been through the Blue-Eyes/Brown-Eyes exercise in my classroom showed significantly less racism in their attitudes than did their Riceville peers. Furthermore, the Riceville students as a whole had expressed less racism in their responses to the survey than did the students in Saint Ansgar. He felt that this was extremely important, as it seemed to prove that not only were my students retaining a great deal of what they'd learned, but their attitudes were rubbing off on their classmates.

From those results I learned a lot about ignorance and fear

and the way to combat both, where racism is concerned: The way to combat it is "ed-u-ca-tion." Not "edgication," but education. The word education is formed from the root duc, duce, which means lead, and the prefix e which means out. To educate someone means to lead them out—of ignorance. The exercise does just that. John Dewey said we learn by doing. John Dewey was right.

11 No One is Immune to the Effects of Discrimination

In the spring of 1971 Bill Peters called me and suggested that the story of the Blue-Eyes/Brown-Eyes exercise might make a marketable book. I thought he was wrong. He persuaded me to come to New York and be interviewed by him so that he could publish a full account of the exercise and its effects. During our first interview he told me that if he wrote the book about the exercise I'd never be able to write one about it. I thought he was wrong. When I read his book and discovered that he'd made no mention of the film Stephen Banker had directed for the Canadian Broadcasting Corporation I thought that was wrong. Peters' book, A Class Divided, didn't sell well; I'm now doing this book; and I don't suppose that Stephen Banker cares about any of this, one way or the other, since he is an eminently sensible man.

When the book was published, Peters and I were sent to "push the book" on several television shows, one of which was the Phil Donahue show in Dayton, Ohio. I had little knowledge of who, or what, Phil Donahue was all about, but both Virginia Graham and Johnny Carson had been so kind when I was on their shows that I was confident that this, too, would be a positive experience, so off we went.

Donahue's studio audience that day was composed of, as I recall, about sixty well dressed, carefully curled, modestly made up white ladies from the ages of thirty to forty-five. I may be wrong about that—it was, after all 26 years ago—but that's the way I remember them. I was seated between Donahue and Peters on a platform in front of these, what I thought looked like intelligent, perceptive women. Donahue introduced us to the audience, told the group a little about what I'd/we'd done, showed some clips of "Eye…" and then invited questions from the audience.

What a question and answer period that was! Some female would ask a question, Donahue would restate the question in "understandable form." I would start to answer; Peters would interrupt and answer for me. On we'd go to the next question from the audience. I finally got out of patience with this sexist silliness and, as Peters began to answer for me yet again, I turned to him and said, "Look, Blue-eyes, I can answer my own questions!" His mouth slammed shut and I answered the question. And Donahue interpreted my answer for the audience. I knew I had struck a nerve in Peters when his face got red, but at that point I'd simply had all the paternalistic behaviors I was willing to tolerate out of those two white males.

We left the studio shortly after the taping and took a cab to the airport en route to Chicago to do the Howard Miller show the next night. Bill had told me several times while interviewing me for the book that he wouldn't be bothered by the Blue-Eyes/Brown-Eyes exercise and he couldn't understand how anyone else would be. However, on the way to the airport, he turned to me and said, "You know what Howard Miller and I are going to do to you tomorrow night, don't you, Jane?"

I said, "No, Bill, what are you going to do?"

He said, "We're going to run the Blue-Eyes/Brown-Eyes exercise on you on camera. Then what'll you do?"

"Well," I answered, "if you do, I'll simply take all the blue-eyed cameramen and walk off the set."

He looked at me and said, "You'd do it, too, wouldn't you?" I said,

"Try me." Then I said, "But Bill, I thought you said you wouldn't be bothered by this exercise. You sound a little bothered to me." We changed the subject. Nobody walked off the set on the Howard Miller show. And I answered my own questions.

12 Is It Coming Around?

In 1971 Darald got a job managing a supermarket in Osage, Iowa, sixteen miles from Riceville. The owner of the store required that we have an Osage address if Darald wanted the job. Darald's first love had been retail sales since he was fourteen years old and worked in his first supermarket, so we bought, and moved into, a remodeled rural schoolhouse six miles from Osage, and Darald went to work. The kids had never before wanted to leave Riceville, because their grandparents, an aunt, an uncle, and several beloved cousins lived there. However, when the time came for this move, they made it with great joy. It wasn't until they and I were sitting around the kitchen table visiting, in our new home one day that I began to understand their joy. That was when they shared with me for the first time some of the really ugly things that were said and done to them on a daily basis by some of the teachers and students in the Riceville school. I was shocked and sickened. I said to them, "Why didn't you tell me this when it was happening? I'd have tried to do something about it."

Sarah said, "We talked about that, but you were having enough trouble as it was. We decided to handle it ourselves."

Brian said, "Anyways if you'd tried to do anything it woulda just made it worse. Don't you worry. Someday I'll get even." Mark nodded in assent.

"Yeah," Mary chimed in. "Remember when Ginnie Gunfighter (their pet name for my father because he reminded them of the heroes in western movies) always says, 'What goes around comes around.' It'll come around."

Will it? Does it? Should it? Has it? I don't know. What I do know is that our four offspring are the kind of people I'd choose for friends, even if they weren't my family. Of course, you need to realize that the people I consider my friends are unique human beings, unconventional and precious and, like diamonds, I hope will last forever.

13 Study the Past in the Present to Prepare for the Future

To leave a lasting monument to the American Revolutionary Bicentennial the Room 10er's decided to build a park called "The Village Green" on a vacant lot on the main street in Riceville. The lot was owned by the bank so we had to get their permission to clean up the lot and plant some trees and erect a sign in it. They gladly gave their permission and we began thinking up ways to make money to finance the project. We did several things. We made Christmas tags out of scrap paper, which we got from a local printing company, and pieces of felt and sold them to whomever would listen to our sales talk. Governor Robert Ray's wife ordered several packs and used them on her Christmas packages that year. We made and sold Christmas cards with haiku verses, which had been made up by the students, on them. In February we made delicate, delicious sugar cookies in the shapes of hearts and feet and sold them in packs of a dozen. On the packaging was written, "We're putting our hearts and soles into the Room 10 Park." Perhaps our slogan wasn't in good taste, but our cookies tasted good. That's another recipe you might want, so here it is.

Foot Cookies:

1 ½ cups powdered sugar	*1 cup butter*
2 ½ cups flour	*1 teaspoon cream of tartar*

1 teaspoon baking soda   1 egg
1 teaspoon vanilla OR ½ teaspoon almond extract

Cream the powdered sugar and the butter. Add the egg and the vanilla. Sift the dry ingredients together. Add them and the vanilla to the creamed mixture. Mix well. Chill. Roll out on floured board. Cut. Bake at 350 degrees for approximately twelve minutes. Watch closely as they get too dark very quickly. Bake until slightly tan.

For several years my students and I collected and sold empty pop and beer cans to make money for our park. Iowa had no bottle law at that time so the roadside ditches were mineral deposits waiting to be mined by anyone who was willing to crawl down and up ditches and pick up smelly, dirty, wet cans; smash them, put them into large plastic garbage bags, and store them until they'd collected a load big enough to take to the nearest recycling center where they could be redeemed for pennies. This was an especially appealing endeavor in the springtime when, in the classroom, a child would stomp on a supposedly empty can and find that it contained the carcass of some furry or scaly creature that had gotten into the can, had frozen in the winter, and had thawed out in the warm classroom. I really don't like spiders and snakes.

While we learned about math and science and reading and ecology, etc. etc., through these projects, we also learned about greed and generosity. The owner of the local telephone company bought the lot for the Room 10 Park out from under us right after we'd purchased and planted our first cherry tree on it. The kids were crushed.

New plan. My parents donated half of the lot on which the hotel stood to become "The Village Green." We planted a honeysuckle hedge to mark the boundaries of the park and constructed – with the help of many of their parents, and my parents and family – a log cabin. My husband and I hauled old telephone poles out of the pole yard up to the site by picking each one up by its large end and sliding it into the back of our station wagon. My husband was a reluctant participant in this endeavor, and I must admit that I wouldn't recommend it as the best way to transport telephone poles.

The third graders and their fathers built that cabin, and when those same students got into seventh grade, they went back to the park and chinked the logs with concrete, since we hadn't had time to do it when they were in the third grade. Six years later, one of those third graders had her picture taken with her bridesmaids in front of that cabin. The cabin is still standing, but some of the fathers who constructed it are dead, including my own. Some of those students' offspring, however, are very much alive, and they play in and around that park and that cabin, spring, summer and fall. They bring furniture and rugs and dishes from their homes, and they sweep the dirt floor and crawl in and out the windows. And one summer, they stood a handmade sign outside the door which read, "Don't mess up the cabin!"

It was in that cabin that my father, on the day before Halloween one year, found stored, in the corner, a whole grocery sack full of cartons of fresh eggs. He took them into the kitchen of the hotel, showed them to my mother and, laughing, said, "Here's what the boys are going to throw tonight." He had seen three or four junior high boys sauntering away from the cabin just before he went outside, and having been the town's hellion as an adolescent, knew just what they intended to do with those eggs. "What'll we do with 'em?" he said.

"Let's boil 'em!" Mom replied. So they did. And put them back in the cartons, and put the cartons back in the sack, and put the sack back in the corner of the cabin. Then, Mom called me and told me what they'd done. My first thought was, "Why didn't I think of that? It's great!" Darald's first reaction to the idea was, "Do you know what a hard-boiled egg will do if it's thrown at a window with enough force?" Oh, shit! I went to school the next morning half in fear and half – well, actually a lot more than half – in anticipation of hearing about the events of the previous evening. The seventh-grade boys congregated in my room and I listened to their conversation as I worked at my desk. Lots of agitation. Lots of bewilderment. Finally I couldn't stand the suspense any longer and I said, "Hey, fellas, did you have fun last night?"

At that they came charging up to my desk and Chad Quinn said, "We got a whole bunch of eggs from Brian's mom yesterday and we left 'em in that little cabin at the Jennison Inn and when I threw one of 'em against a house last night it didn't' splat; it just made a 'thud' and fell on the ground!"

"Yeah, well," another said, "I threw one at a cat and it almost killed it!"

"That's nothin'," said another. "You hit me on the arm with one and darned near broke my arm! That hurt!"

At that point, Chad turned to Brian, from whose mother they'd gotten the eggs, and demanded, "Just how many eggs does your mother cook at one time, anyway Brian?" Poor Brian. He had no explanation and none of them thought to connect me to the Jennison Inn, so I thought we were home free. Not so.

That night Chad's grandmother called my mother at the Jennison Inn and asked, "Gie, were those three- or four-minute eggs that you boiled yesterday?" No windows got broken and no paint jobs were ruined by raw eggs that Halloween night, but lots of people had to pick eggshells out of the bushes around their foundations, and there was at least one Riceville feline that wasn't feelin' so good.

14 We Have Sown the Wind

I continued to teach at the elementary level in Riceville until 1977, at which time one of the junior high teachers retired and they were going to put one of the kindergarten teachers into that position. I'd been teaching third grade for long enough, in my opinion, and I knew that the teacher they were sending up to the junior high would be eaten alive by those seventh and eighth graders; she was so sweet you could get candy coated by standing next to her, and they were a group of big, "tough," tyrannical kids. I applied for the junior high job. The elementary principal, Leonard Crawford, who had replaced our dear Dinsmore Brandmill, was also the junior high principal and was tickled pink at my suggestion. Of course we had to take the idea up to the school superintendent, Dean Weaver, who had been hired upon Mr. Johnston's retirement. His response to telling him that I wanted to make the move was, "Good. You're the one we wanted to send, but we couldn't ask you to go because you've got so much seniority. You've got the job." Later that same day I told the janitor about my plans for the coming year and, since he was also the junior high building janitor, when he went to work at the junior high building that day he told the seventh and eighth grade students about my intentions for the coming year.

They responded to the news by telling him, "You go back down there and tell her that if she comes up here, we'll throw her out the third-story window." Naturally, being the sweet, thoughtful guy he was he rushed right back and gave me the message.

"Fine," I said, "They can probably throw me out because they're all bigger than I am, but you go back and tell them that they're going to have to figure out what they're going to do with me when I come back up those stairs."

"Oh, shit," the boys said when they got my message, "She will, too. We'll have to figure out something else…" And they did. When they stepped into my classroom that year they were so saintly you could hear their wings rustle as they prepared to sit down. A more absolutely delightful group than those students were I've never known.

We did, however, have some wild moments. Some of the eighth-grade boys in that group were into grabbing, pushing, and shoving the girls. One of them chased a girl into my classroom, and while he was standing there arguing with her while facing me, I reached up, grabbed the front of his jacket with both hands, slipped my right foot behind his right foot and, while jerking him forward with my left hand, pushed him backward with my right hand and hip and dropped him with one smooth movement. I don't know who was more surprised, the big, tough guy or me. I didn't let him go, just held him about four inches off the floor and, looking down at his shocked and actually delighted countenance, said, while shaking him slightly, "Now, are you ever going to bother her again?"

"No! No!" he said. "Let me up!" I pulled him upright and watched him while he straightened his blue denim jacket, all the time keeping a wary eye on me. "Elliott," he said, "how'd you do that? Will you teach it to me?"

I laughed and said, "Oh, no. I'm afraid you'd use it on some girl."

He left, grinning, and as he went down the hall I heard him say to someone, "Jeez, you should see what Elliott can do. You better be careful around her." Sarah was taking self-defense classes for her physical education major at UNI at that time and had taught me that one move. She'd told me never to drop the person I used it on unless I wanted to hurt them, so I was careful to hold onto that one. And I never used that trick again.

Because the wrestling coaches in the Riceville athletic department compared the members of the boys' basketball team to women, the word "woman" became a frequent taunt used by male students to belittle their male peers in that system. I asked the principal, Steven Harnack (Mr. Crawford had resigned at the end of the previous year), to try to put a stop to that odious practice. No results.

I was working near the door of my classroom one day and heard a tall, skinny semi-tough boy say to some other male in the hall, "Ah, you woman, you."

I took about four giant strides to where he was standing, grabbed him by the front of his jacket, slammed him up against the lockers behind him and, looking way, way up said through clenched teeth, "Don't you ever use that word as a swear word in this hallway, again! Do you understand me?"

"Yeah! Yeah! Jeez, Elliott, what're ya doin?" He asked in shock and confusion.

"Do you understand me?" I ground out again.

"Yeah, yeah, I'm sorry," he said, "It won't happen again." I felt like a fool: The kid had to look way down to see me! But I got the message across.

It didn't change the wrestling coaches' approach to motivation but it did alter that student's hall behaviors. I wish it had changed the coaches' attitudes, particularly since so many of our administrators are former coaches. It is difficult to raise non-sexist young men if they are constantly being conditioned by their elders and some of their adult role models to the idea that women are inferior and powerless beings who are there to be used and/or abused, verbally and physically.

While I was teaching at the elementary level it had become my awful habit as I drove the thirteen miles from school to home at night, particularly after some nastier-than-usual behavior on the part of my peers, to imagine myself blowing the offender off the face of the earth. Several years after I'd been at the junior high, I was walking through the hall of the elementary building one afternoon and I saw one of those whom I had disposed of coming toward me.

"What are you doing here?" I wondered in surprise. "I thought I'd killed you." I was saddened by my response to seeing her in the hall that day, but I was even more upset when I heard that one of those who had taken savage delight, it seemed to me, in the "Dirty Tricks" game, was dying. You see, I didn't feel any sympathy for her pain and suffering. I had so dehumanized myself where some of my peers were concerned that their agony was meaningless to me. I didn't rejoice in their misery; I just flat out didn't care. What if this is what happens in the psyches of those we, in the majority in this country, mistreat on a daily basis? How long can we mistreat people, either our peers and neighbors, or strangers, and still expect them to care when we are in pain? What if women come to feel about men the way men seem to feel about women? And what if people of color come to feel about whites the way most whites seem to feel about them? We are indeed sowing the wind and we will surely reap the whirlwind.

Now some psychologist is going to analyze my behavior and write a thesis about the effect on students of having an out-of-control, middle aged woman teaching at the junior high level. Go ahead. Write your paper, but don't do what so many college students do: Don't write to me and ask me to help you do your research.

15 As the Twig is Bent

In the winter of 1984 the students who had been filmed by
ABC in 1970 called me and told me that they were coming back
to Riceville for their 5-year class reunion. Would I bring The Eye
of the Storm to the reunion and show it to them? Yes! I hadn't
seen them as a group since they were in my third grade class and
I needed to talk to them.

I immediately called Bill Peters and said, "They're coming
back!" He didn't ask who was coming back.

He said,"When will they be there?" I told him the date of the
reunion and he said, "We'll be there with a film crew." He
contacted ABC and as I understand it, the other major networks,
and offered them the opportunity to film this event. They weren't
interested in covering the reunion, said it was "old news." An
oxymoron if ever I heard one. Sort of like George Carlin's
'jumbo shrimp' and' military intelligence;' and my seventh
graders' 'awfully nice' and 'President Reagan', which is my
favorite of all. As a last resort he contacted PBS and was
successful in selling them on the idea of filming the reunion.

Bill Peters, the PBS film crew, eleven of the original sixteen
"Eye..." stars, some of their mates and their children, and I met
in the lobby of the Riceville Community School on Saturday,
August 11, 1984. They were all even more remarkable than I'd

remembered. We hugged and held and laughed a lot and cried a little and talked a bit about those who'd been unable to attend for one reason or another: about Russell Ring who had been killed in an accident two weeks before high school graduation, and about John Benttine who had been injured in an automobile accident after high school and was a paraplegic. I was in awe of this group. Here were Sheila Schaefer with her husband and their children. Sandy Dohlman, Donna Reddel, Susan Ginder, Julie Smith brought their children, for God's sake! They'd all been children the last time I saw them. Verla Buls, was taller than I and beautiful. Milton Wolthoff, who was still smiling and ducking his head in that delightful way; and Brian Saltou, who wasn't arguing about anything. Roy Wilson, spent the night sleeping in his pickup outside the school, after driving all the way from southern Missouri to be there. Rex Kozak and Raymond Hansen, whom I'd seen over the years, but never before as my peers. I knew that most of these kids had gone farther and done more in the past thirteen years than I had in my first thirty-six years and I could only marvel at what I saw in that group.

After our initial greetings, we went into a classroom in the high school section of the building, where cameras and sound equipment and lights and a sixteen millimeter sound projector and screen had been set up in preparation for our viewing <u>The Eye of the Storm</u>. I had watched the film with the crew the day before as they prepared their lighting and sound equipment. The members of the crew, most of whom were young, Jewish males, had never seen the film before, so they had to run it in order to get a feel for the acoustics and lighting in the room. At one point during the viewing I heard a strange noise behind me and turned to see one of the film crew members sitting up against the wall, crying.

When the film was over he came to where I was sitting and said, "Mrs. Elliott, I have to talk to you out in the hall." I followed him out the door and a short way down the hall, where he stopped and said to me, "There's something I want you to have." He reached into the back pocket of his jeans, and took out his billfold. Out of it he took a small yellow square of folded cloth. As he began to unfold the cloth he said to me, "I'm Jewish. My father was one of the one thousand survivors of his ghetto during the Hitler years. He used to describe to me what happened to the Jews during the Holocaust, but I never understood what he was talking about until I saw your film. I want to thank you for helping me to understand what my father was trying to tell me. I want you to have this." He unfolded the frayed yellow square of cloth and held it out to me. In the middle of that yellow cloth was drawn a black outline of the Star of David and across that Star of David was written the word, 'Jude.'

I gasped. "Is this what I think it is?" I asked.

He said, "It's the patch my father had to wear in the ghetto. I want you to have the patch."

I was thunderstruck. I said, "I want that patch more than life itself but I can't take it. Someday you'll find someone who truly deserves that patch, but I'm not the one. Please keep it. But thank you for the loveliest compliment I've ever received."

Now, you have to know that something strange has just happened here. I had forgotten that event in the last few years and so had no intention of including it in this narrative. Describing the day triggered my memory of that moment. I have thought as I've been writing this thing that someone will probably ask me whether writing this book has been a sort of catharsis for me. I was prepared to answer, "Not really," but I didn't know why that would be my answer.

Now I know. This isn't purging the pain resulting from the experiences I've had, or erasing the sadness resulting from the things I've seen and heard: It's dredging them up and forcing me to look at them and relate to what they mean all over again. Damn!

The Jews say, 'If you don't know what hurts me, you cannot really love me.' What that young Jewish male's father knows, I will never know, but I think that now I understand more than I did before. I'm not sure I'm grateful for the understanding. I'm not less angry, disgusted, or impatient with the irrational behaviors of some of the members of my community, my profession, my neighbors, my society, my family, my religion, and myself: If anything, I'm more angry.

We know better, so why don't we do better? Because we choose not to! We choose to perpetuate these racist behaviors and policies. We choose to nominate and elect bigoted officials. We choose to follow homophobic leaders and to watch sexist television commercials and to support hate-mongering radio and television talk-show hosts. We choose to support an educational system which perpetuates the myth of white supremacy in a country where over twenty-five per cent of the population is other than white and has shown ample proof, by succeeding in spite of all the obstacles we place in their path, just how mistaken a myth it is. We're making bad choices for our present and for our children's future. Catharsis? More like re-injury.

We watched the film together that August day and the former students laughed all the way through it. After all, they'd been nine years old when the film was made and they hadn't seen it in fourteen years. When the film ended they said,

"Can you run it again? We didn't hear what we were saying." So the film was rewound and we watched it again. The second time through some of the members of the group cried as they watched their own nine-year-old faces and some argued with the teacher on the screen. They didn't address their remarks to me in person, only to the teacher on the screen. It was a very strange experience to be, but not be, in that situation. When the film ended for the second time, we turned on the lights, arranged our chairs in a circle, and began to discuss what we'd just seen and how we felt as we saw it. If I had written the script for that discussion I couldn't have composed anything more gratifying to me or anything more supportive of the exercise than what they expressed in the next few hours. I would never have dared to imagine that these young people would make the following statements concerning the eye-color experience in response to my questions:

Question: Did I do you a graver disservice than a service by using the eye-color exercise with you in third grade?

Raymond: Mrs. Elliott, a great Greek philosopher once said, 'The unexamined life isn't worth living.' You made my life worth living. I have to re-examine my life every day. (At that time Raymond was a paralegal working in the Cook County Courthouse in Chicago, Illinois) Every day I have to ask myself, 'Am I relating to the color here, or to the case?'

Question (to Sandy): Has having this exercise changed how you live your life at all?

Sandy: Every time I hear one of those bigoted remarks, I wish I had one of those collars in my pocket and I could whip that collar out and put it around that person's neck and say, "Now you wear that collar for two weeks and see how you'd like to live that way for a lifetime."

Rex: I can't get that collar out of my pocket. I'll have

that collar in my pocket for the rest of my life.

Question (to Sandy's husband): What's it like to be married to someone who had this exercise when she was in third grade?

Sandy's husband: I'm glad I married someone who had you for a teacher because our children aren't being raised the way my nieces and nephews are: When Sandy hears one of those bigoted remarks she makes the child who said it sit down and she explains to him or her why we don't say those things in our house. Not only have you changed the kind of person Sandy is; you've changed the kind of person I am, the kind of people our children will be, and the kind of people our grandchildren will be. I'm honored to be married to someone who had you for a teacher.

Question: What's wrong with the exercise?

Raymond: The only thing wrong with the exercise is not enough teachers are using it. Every child should have to go through that exercise at some time in their school career because it literally changes the kind of person you become (The group agreed that this was the way they all felt.).

Roy: It changes the kind of person you are. Even in our homes we was better people.

Verla: When you see people doing these things now, it boggles up inside you and you remember how it felt.

Susan: When I see Blacks doing something now I think, "Well, it's because they're...", and I don't even finish the thought. I tell myself that I see lots of whites and others doing the same thing. It's just because they're black that I'm noticing.

At noon, the former students and their families left the

building to attend the picnic being held by the entire class at the lake north of town.

When they returned to the school for interviews and pictures after the picnic, Sandy came up to me and said, "Well, it happened again, Mrs. Elliott."

"What do you mean, Sandy? What happened?" I asked her, dreading the answer. She then related how, as she was sitting at the picnic table eating lunch – after the non-Room 10 class member had insisted that the camera crews leave the area! – one of the classmates who had been in the accelerated group throughout his school years in Riceville, leaned across the table and said to her, "Why are they doing a film about your group? You were the dummy group! Ours was the group that should have been filmed!"

"Sandy, I'm sorry," I said. "But what did you say to him?"

Sandy actually laughed as she shrugged her shoulders and said, "He isn't as smart as he thinks he is. He still hasn't learned what we know." I was so proud of her aplomb and so in awe of her maturity. My first impulse, if that had happened to me, would have been to make some vicious, cutting remark – or dump his plate over his head – but Sandy simply recognized his ignorance and kept right on keepin' on.

16 The Village Dogs Bark, But the Caravan Moves On

The footage of that reunion became part of a film entitled <u>A Class Divided</u> which was shown on PBS in the fall. As a result of that exposure a black female employee of the Mountain Bell Telephone Company in Denver, Colorado, called me and asked me if I'd do fifteen Blue-Eyes/Brown-Eyes exercises with the employees of several corporations in the Denver area the following year. I told her that I'd have to clear that with the school's administrators.

First I went to the principal, Steve Harnack, and asked him for fifteen days of unpaid professional leave to work with corporations during the year. I told him that I'd do all the preparation and planning for my substitute before I left each time; I'd do all the correcting and grading of the work the students had done in my absence when I came back, and that I'd teach my substitute how to teach Orton/Gillingham Phonics so that, if I had the opportunity to do the exercise full time with corporations at the end of the year, they'd have a trained tutor to take my place—and at no extra cost to the school district. This sounded great to Mr. Harnack, but he said we'd have to take the proposal to the superintendent, Norm Kolberg. We did. He agreed with our plan, but said that the proposal would have to be presented to the board of education for their approval. He wanted me to be at the board meeting to answer any questions that board members might have. I agreed to do that, so they included the plan to have me pitch this thing to the board in the proposed agenda for the next board meeting. The agenda, as usual, was published in the local paper that week. Someone must have read the article to the members of the Riceville Education Association because they immediately sent a representative to the superintendent to inform him that my appearance before the board and my taking unpaid professional leave were not covered in the Master Contract so they were going to protest that. They also said that if I was allowed to take unpaid professional leave, it would "set an unfortunate precedent" as the board would expect all the teachers to take unpaid professional leave in the future. Therefore, if we went ahead with our plan for me to meet with the board, the REA would file a grievance against the board. In fact, since what we were proposing wasn't mentioned in the Master Contract, we had every right to do what we had planned, but I was fed up with their petty puling (look it up) and I told the principal – in typically tactful fashion – that they should put the Master Contract where the sun doesn't shine and that I'd take a hundred and eighty days of unpaid professional leave. Which I did, but not until I'd interviewed the candidates for my position, had chosen my replacement, and had agreed to come back and teach that person how to use Orton/Gillingham Phonics with dyslexic readers.

I can hear your mental wheels turning as you ask yourself some questions right now. Here are some of the questions I think you have in your mind and some of the answers I have in mine.

Question: Why did you stay and teach in Riceville as long as you did?

Answer: Where would I go? I had lots of seniority and lots of education and no other school was going to want to afford to hire me for the salary I was getting at that time in Riceville. Furthermore, the Riceville School wasn't the only one ruled by racism: What other school administrators would voluntarily hire someone with my record for challenging the status quo?

Question: Why didn't they fire you long before this?

Answer: That was one of the questions an interviewer asked Superintendent Johnston and he replied, "In my heart of hearts I knew she was right. How could I fire someone for doing the right thing?" New school board members got elected several times during my tenure at Riceville because of their promise to fire the school's "nigger lover" but, since superintendents, and not boards of education, have the authority to hire and fire teachers, I never really worried about being fired after that first exercise.

Question: Didn't anyone in Riceville support you?

Answer: You don't understand how racism works. If other people had publicly defended me, those who were opposed to what I was doing would have turned on my defenders and treated them as they were treating me. It's called intimidation, and it works, particularly with people who greatly desire the acceptance and approval of their peers. However, Elaine Eschweiler and Eleanor Benjegerdes, two of the school secretaries, stand out in my memory of that experience like oak trees in a patch of bullthistles. They gave a whole new meaning to the words professional behavior.

Question: What about your parents and your siblings? How did they react to what you were doing?

Answer: In various ways. My father sent clippings to his sisters about what I was doing; my mother told me I sounded like her aunt Eunice, who spent her last years in a mental institution; my sisters, Mary and Jean, have been unfailingly accepting of the exercise; and my brothers' reactions have pretty much depended on their financial situations and their political affiliations at any given time. Being the relative of the town's "nigger lover" couldn't have been easy.

Question: Have people's opinions of you changed over the years?

Answer: I don't think so. But since only twenty percent of the parents in Riceville objected strongly to having their children placed in my classrooms, I have to think that the other eighty percent, while not eager to stand up and defend me, were at least not willing to brand the scarlet R for Radical on my forehead, either. And I had absolutely splendid cooperation from most of the parents of my students every year that I taught in that system. No matter what I asked of them they came through. Bad parents aren't usually known for producing good children, and the children I taught in Riceville weren't just good, they were fantastic!

Question: Why wasn't any of the unpleasantness that you and your family experienced as a result of the exercise mentioned in A Class Divided, the book by William Peters?

Answer: Because I was still reacting like a victim when Bill Peters interviewed me. I was still convinced that if strangers knew how some of the people in Riceville felt about me, the strangers too would think I was a bad person. For a while I thought I must have done a really terrible thing for so many people to hate me, but several years ago, I finally realized that I hadn't done a bad thing. There was nothing wrong with what I'd done, but there was something very wrong with how some people reacted to it. At that moment I stopped acting like a victim and stopped protecting the victimizers.

Question: Why don't you just leave out the parts about the anger and the brutish behaviors? Telling those things just turns people off. This book would be much more positive and uplifting if you'd just tell about the good things that happened.

Answer: And it would also be a lie. To omit the ugly facts would be to do what white folks have been doing in this country at least since 1980 and the election of Ronald Reagan to the presidency: We've been trying to convince ourselves that by ignoring "the problem" we can make it disappear. We should know better. The evil of racism is like a cancer; if you ignore it, it will continue to grow and will finally consume you. If you hire learned scholars to come in and look at it and just talk about it, it will finally consume you. If you say that it's just God's way and periodically pray for it to be cured, it will finally consume you. If you wait for someone else to come along and solve your problem, because you feel powerless to do anything, your cancer will finally consume you. However, racism and cancer are dissimilar in one very important way: There is a cure for racism!

Perhaps the readers of this book will become more aware of their own language and behaviors, and will become less tolerant of those who use racist language and exhibit racist behaviors in their presence. Perhaps white people will see themselves as people of color see them, while reading this book, and will decide to change their behaviors so as not to be perceived as I've perceived some of those with whom I've had to associate through these sometimes less than pleasant years. We can't change the mistakes we've made in the past, but we can stop making those same mistakes in the present and, by so doing, construct a much more positive future. Members of Alcoholics Anonymous say that the mark of insanity is doing the same thing over and over and expecting different results. It's time to begin the process of changing our language and our behaviors. And the first step in that process is to identify, recognize, and admit the mistakes of the past instead of rationalizing them, denying them, or trying to cover them up. You want a nice book? Try Rebecca of Sunnybook Farm. But remember, if you quit reading at this point, that reality is not always pretty and that racism never is. In writing this I'm describing what I encountered as a result of working to decrease the level of racism in this society. What I encountered was racism. It wasn't pretty.

Question: When you needed fifteen days to work with corporations why didn't you just take fifteen days of sick leave and keep your job? You had sick leave coming, didn't you?

Answer: Of course. By 1984 I had ninety days of accumulated sick leave, but to take sick leave without being sick would have been dishonest as well as unethical. That suggestion was made to me at the time and I rejected it.

Question: Why didn't you just take paid professional leave and contribute the wages you made, on those days, to the school?

Answer: I didn't think it would be ethical to be paid for work I wasn't doing and when I made that suggestion to Superintendent Kolberg he wouldn't approve it. It would have made for some interesting bookkeeping problems, wouldn't it?

Question: What's your greatest regret when you look back on those years in Riceville?

Answer: Obviously, my greatest anger is over what my fellow teachers and some of their students did to my offspring. My greatest regret is the years when, out of just plain weariness with the wickedness, I didn't do the exercise with my students. By not doing it I did those students a disservice in that I withheld from them some important knowledge that would have been helpful to them in the future.

Question: What's your best memory of your Riceville experience?

Answer: We celebrated the American Revolution Bicentennial big time (Now, if you aren't particularly interested in kids and classes and education you might want to skip this portion of the book.). We started in 1972 and never stopped until 1976. In 1972 we did lots of creative dramatics around the subject of the ARB. One of the events we dramatized was the Boston Tea Party. My nephew, Tim Yager, was one of the patriots who was arrested and thrown into jail during the dramatization. When he described to his mother at home that night how he and the others were trying to dig their way out of jail by tunneling through the floor, his little sister, who was in first grade and was listening to his description, said, "Mom, do they really have dirt floors in Mrs. Elliott's room?" Tim really got into creative dramatics.

On April 18th of 1975 we reenacted Paul Revere's ride (creatively). We held auditions for the part of Paul Revere during the previous week. Todd Koenigs got the part and, with the principal's permission, during the last half hour of school on that day, he ran through the halls with leaflets in his hands, knocking on classroom doors and, when the teachers answered the doors, thrusting a sheaf of leaflets into their hands, while yelling at the top his lungs, "To arms! To arms! The British are coming! The British are coming!" You think the Minutemen got into trouble! Such anger! Not, however, on the part of everyone. When he opened the door to the Superintendent's office, shouted out his warning, and threw the leaflets on the floor, we weren't aware that the Board of Education was in session there. Of course they were all startled by the interruption and questioned Mr. Weaver as to what was going on.

"Oh," he explained, "it's just some of Mrs. Elliott's students and their Revolutionary War activities." When Todd came galloping back to the room, gasping and out of breath, he collapsed onto a chair and said,

"Boy, Mrs. Elliott, I know just what Paul Revere felt like when he was bein' chased by the British! Miss L___ and Miss ___ both tried to catch me and keep me from goin' on! But I got away!" His peers cheered. My peers pouted.

17 Are Adults Just Big Children?

Darald was more than a little worried when I decided to quit teaching and go out on my own. His concerns were legitimate and his questions logical. My answers were....mine.

Question: Why would you give up a sure thing to take a chance on the word of someone you don't even know?

Answer: Because this is a great chance.

Question: What if it doesn't work?

Answer: What if it does?

Question: Dammit, Jane, that's no answer! What'll we do after you've done the first fifteen workshops? You don't even have a contract with these people.

Answer: If it ends I'll find a job doing something else. Or you can hire me to work for you (I knew that suggestion would thrill him to death!).

Question: What if someone decides to sue for the discrimination during the exercise? What will you do then?

Answer: The exercise is part of a 3-day workshop provided by the corporations. They are liable for any damages; I'm not. And besides, if someone sues a corporation for damage that they suffer as a result of the discrimination during this workshop, it will give every person of color, every homosexual, every female, every person with a disability, and every white male, as well as all those whose religious holidays are not observed by that corporation, the right to sue for discrimination. Do you really think these corporations are going to let that happen?

Question: What if someone decides to wipe you out? Remember what happened in Uniontown? (Several years previous to this discussion three carloads of Blacks had escorted me and Anna S. Cunningham out of Uniontown and as far as the Pennsylvania Turnpike after ten o'clock at night, because some of several hundred teachers whom we had put through a very informal version of the exercise in the morning called the superintendent of schools in the afternoon and told him, as it was quoted to me, "You'd better get that bitch out of town or we're gonna shoot her.")

Answer: Yes, I remember, Darald, but think about it: If somebody shoots me they'll make an instant martyr of me. Do you really think anyone's dumb enough to risk having to celebrate Jane Elliott Day for the rest of their lives?

Question: What about me? Jane Elliott Day once a year won't do me any good. I'd rather have Jane Elliott for lots of days and nights.

Answer: That's a lovely sentiment and I appreciate it, but here's what we'll do to help you through that dilemma: I'll take out a large life and disability insurance policy. Then, if something happens and they kill me, you and the kids will have something to remember me by. If they don't shoot straight and I'm disabled we'll have something to get along on. Just give me three years. If I can do this for three years we can put away enough to buy a small business near Mary in San Diego and be reasonably comfortable without my teaching. Look, I realize that it's a risk, but someone has said, "Nothing can stop a man with a dream or an idea whose time has come." I'm not a man, but I've got a dream, and perhaps this idea's time has come.

I went to work with Linda Guillory at Mountain Bell and Public Service of Colorado in Denver, Colorado. The Blue-Eyed/Brown-Eyed exercise was the middle day of a three day workshop. I did the exercise with Mountain Bell—which became US West during the time I worked with them—for three years and with US West Direct for four years. After the first two years, Linda decided to conduct workshops for PSCo without me and went out on her own. US West and US West Direct, however, continued to use BE/BE as the middle day of their training for some time. I have several very vivid memories of workshops we did for US West, PSCo, and Direct.

For the first exercise we did for one of the corporations, I should have received combat pay. A number of the blue-eyed white males in the group were Human Resources people who had been doing workshops for the company for some time and were not about to allow themselves to be manipulated by one small insignificant white female and one large angry black one. Therefore, they refused to listen to anything the facilitators said (we blamed their refusal on their eye color and gave them no recognition); they refused to sit where they were told (once again, they were reacting because of their eye color); they refused to wear the collars as they were instructed to (When one of them pinned his on his rear end and pranced around waving it like a tail we blamed it on his eye color.); they refused to hand in their papers when told to (One got into a tug of war with me over his paper. I won.); and they refused to leave the room when they were instructed to do so, (since they couldn't understand and follow directions). At this point these two blue-eyed boys got up on one of the tables and commenced to dance as they believed Blacks dance. That was going too far. Linda and I took the Brown-eyed people to another room and left the miscreant "Blueys" in the room which they had trashed. The "good Blueys" went with the Browns, taking the bad boys entire audience with them. There was no way the bad boys could win in this situation and they finally realized it when we refused them entry into the workshop's new location. They were effectively out of the workshop. Several months later one of the delinquents wrote an honest and forthright description of his experience that day, in the in-house newsletter. He and one of his cohorts later became facilitators and ardent supporters of the exercise.

I learned a lot on that first exercise. I had allowed the room for that first exercise to be arranged as it would traditionally be done in corporate training session at that time: Tables, pitchers of water, glasses, pencils and paper, a secure environment. Never again! After that I got rid of the tables: No more dancing space! I put the blue-eyed people in pairs on uncomfortable folding chairs in the center of the room facing the front of the room, thereby "ghettoizing" them. I put the Brown-eyes in comfortable chairs facing the center of the room on each side of the Blue group so that we could keep the Blues under constant supervision. I provided enough chairs for only one-half the Blues, thereby forcing part of them to sit on the floor, which provided different positions of power between members of the group and prevented any opportunities for bonding between them. When I saw bonding beginning to happen, I moved people from the chairs to the floor, thereby letting them know that making friends would be perceived as plotting against the power structure, which wasn't going to be tolerated. I replaced the large hand-drawn posters which we'd used at the first workshop – someone had disposed of the entire set "accidentally" – with ever more offensive ones and insisted that the Blues stand individually to read the signs aloud at the beginning of each session. Revolt is difficult when you are being required to stand and read signs about people like yourself, which say things like:

Is it true Browns have more fun?

Let in one blue-eye and there goes the neighborhood.

I'm not prejudiced; some of my best friends are blue-eyed.

Eenie, meenie, minie, mo, catch a Bluey by the toe.

If I have but one life to live, let me live it as a brown.

If Blueys don't like it here, why don't they go back where they came from?

And the ever popular:

Would you want your daughter to marry one?

Blueys take exception to the sentiments expressed on the signs themselves, but having to read them aloud and then being criticized for the way they read them aloud, is adding insult to injury. And, to top it all off, their fumbling, mumbling, stuttering, stammering, anger, and frustration are blamed on their eye color instead of on the way they're being treated. By the time they've read the last sign, the answer to the first one is definitely, "Yes!" Browns, obviously, are having a lot more fun and will do almost anything; it seems, to maintain the status quo.

After the signs have been read I tell the blue participants that they obviously aren't paying attention and I try to help them to do that by teaching them the "physical aspects of the listening skills." This is an excellent opportunity to prove to the participants that all our preconceptions about Blueys are true as they, for the most part, prove themselves unable to satisfactorily write four simple sentences that any third grader can write and learn in twenty minutes flat.

After spending several minutes – sometimes as much as an hour – getting the Blueys to write the four sentences correctly, I test them on their retention of the material. Naturally, they all fail the test.

Then I tell them the rules of the day, which are only necessitated by their presence in the workshop. When they seem reluctant to accept the fact that they are as disgusting and depraved as I have accused them of being, I simply use a twisted history of the last four hundred years in this country to prove the validity of my claims. The history is "twisted" only in that it paints Blueys as the villains and Browns as the heroes, just as the history we teach in most of the schools in this country defines white people as the heroes and those "others" as the villains, or perhaps worse yet, hapless victims who were too ignorant and uncivilized to know how to properly use the land and its resources, and so had to be taught the best (white) way to attain not only health, happiness, and prosperity, but also eternal salvation. After about half an hour of this conditioning-masquerading-as-education, I give the participants a culturally biased test which the Blueys can't possibly pass, have the Browns correct all the papers, and then read the scores aloud. Obviously, the Blueys' low scores are blamed on their genetic inferiority and not on the situation which we have created for them.

At this point each participant is told to write three adjectives describing how the people in the other group looked to them during the exercise. The Blues write how the Browns looked, and the Browns write how the Blues looked. After all are finished writing, the words are read and discussed. Then each person writes a short paragraph telling what he/she has learned during the exercise which she/he didn't know before. After a short break for rest and recuperation we come back to the chairs, which are now arranged in a circle and we discuss what took place, internally and externally, during the exercise.

After my first exercise at one of the large corporations I was told by the head of the Human Resources department that in the future they would have a psychologist in the meeting room to help participants to deal with any psychological trauma they might experience during the exercise.

"Oh," I said, "and do you have a psychologist in each department in your corporation to help white women and all people of color to deal with the psychological trauma they may experience in the workplace every day?"

"Well," she replied, "they can meet with the psychologist if they need to."

"With no stigma attached?" I asked.

"Well, I can't guarantee that," she answered.

"Okay, here's what I'm going to do," I told her. "I'm going to introduce the psychologist which you place in this room to the participants and tell them why she's here."

"Oh," she sighed, "you wouldn't do that."

"Try me," I said.

"All right," she said, "I'll station her in a room down the hall and we can send anyone who needs her down there."

"And I'll announce to the participants that she's there, and why," I warned.

"Well," she said, "I just feel that it's necessary that we do this and I guess you feel that it's necessary that you do that." So she put the psychologist in a room down the hall from the meeting place and I told the participants that the psychologist was available. None of the participants availed themselves of her services and three workshops later, they stopped bringing her in. Her presence was offensive to many of us in that it sent the message to minority-group members that their daily and continuing psychological abuse in the workplace was less important to the corporation than was this once-in-a-workshop two-and-a-half-hour psychological discomfort for whites, particularly males.

During one of the early exercises at a large corporation a blue-eyed male dressed in classic casual wear came in with his little tennis sweater tied nattily around his shoulders, his hands jauntily shoved in his front pants pockets, his nearly white hair beautifully coifed, and his smile perfectly practiced. He was cute! When it was his turn to register, he signed in under "Non-Brown", of course, and commenced to behave the way most Blueys do during the exercise: He gave his chair to a lady, resisted sitting on the floor, sat down under protest, read the signs badly, made mistakes (but not many) in writing the listening skills, was generally uncomfortable during the history lesson, but got a good score on the culturally biased test. When we read the scores aloud, he and those people sitting on the floor around him all had scores of from 13 to 17 out of a possible 26 points. As each blue-eyed person's name was read and their score was announced by the Brown who had corrected their test the Bluey was told to go and get his/her paper from the one who had corrected it. When it came time for the cute blue man to get his test he merely leaned forward and held out his hand, snapping his fingers indicating that the brown-eyed female who had corrected his test should either stretch forward or get up to bring it to him. I immediately attacked him.

"Who do you think you are?" I demanded. "Get up off your butt, Bobby Baby, and go get that paper. You need all the exercise you can get." There was a rustle of nervous giggling at this point but not until several minutes later did I understand why. After he had gotten his paper and was back on the floor I said,

"You cheated on this test, didn't you?"

"No!" he responded, in righteous indignation. "I didn't have to cheat. I'm familiar with this material."

"That may be," I retorted, "but how do you explain the fact that everyone around you got high scores and none of those Blueys sitting on chairs did? You cheated on this test!"

"I did not cheat," he insisted. "I might have shared answers but I didn't cheat!" At this the nervous giggles among the Browns became delighted guffaws. And I suddenly realized that the blue boy whose name I had been mispronouncing was the CEO of the company. When we got in to the circle for the debriefing I announced that I'd enjoyed working with this corporation, but that I probably wouldn't be working with them in the future in view of my treatment of their CEO. At that, the CEO leaned forward in his chair, looked me directly in the eye and said,

"You did it exactly right, Ms. Elliott. I didn't want to be treated any differently than the Blue-Eyes were." The group applauded. I breathed a giant sigh of relief. At the end of the debriefing when I collected the green collars from the Blueys he refused to give his up. When I asked why he wouldn't surrender it, he said,

"Because I don't ever want to forget what I earned here today." He later told one of the facilitators of the exercise that he had attached the collar to the mirror over his bureau and, he said, "That's the first thing I see when I get dressed every morning. I get reinforced in what I learned in that exercise every day." Even though the experience had been cold and cruel, he continued to fund the BE/BE exercise for the rest of the time he headed that corporation.

By the time I'd done the exercise for several years in one corporation, word got out, of course, about the danger of having blue eyes during the workshop and people would come to the workshop either cocked and primed to go off, in the case of some white males; or intimidated and anxiety-ridden, in the case of some white females; or eager and curious to see what was the cause of the enthusiastic reactions to the workshop which they'd seen and heard from their peers, in the case of people of color. The reactions of one group of participants stands out most clearly in my mind.

Whenever we did the exercise we kept the meeting room door closed until all the participants had registered so that no one could come into the room and get information about what was going to happen and so forewarn the Blues. On the morning of this exercise we had put the signs up and otherwise prepared the room and I was in the room "readying my remarks" – actually saying my regular prayer for guidance and wisdom – when a young, clean-cut arrogant blue-eyed white male opened the door and, with his jacket in his hand, stepped into the room.

"Good morning," he said, as he started across the room.

"Wait outside until we're ready for you," I said.

"I'm going to hang up my jacket," he said as he proceeded

across the room.

"Don't hang up that jacket. You're to stay outside until we're ready for you," I said.

"I'm hanging up my jacket," he said as he hung his jacket on the coat rack and headed for the door at that end of the room. I followed him to the coat rack and, as he left the room and started down the hall, I took his jacket from its hanger, walked out the door and down the hall behind him and dropped his jacket on the floor at the end of the registration table outside the meeting room door. He heard it hit the floor – it was leather and rather nice, for something owned by a Bluey – and turned and said to me,

"If somebody steals my jacket because of you, you're going to be in big trouble."

"I'm not responsible for taking care of your jacket," I said. "You should have kept it with you. Follow the rules in the future." He left the jacket lying on the floor and stomped down the hall as I went back into the meeting room. This is how my prayers usually get answered? I should stop praying!

A short time later, when the facilitators brought the participants to line-up in the hall preparatory to registering for the day, there were of course lots of questions asked about the jacket on the floor. I simply said that some blue-eyed fool hadn't followed the rule again; you know how they are. That explanation didn't make the blues very comfortable, but the browns began to grin. When the owner (shoplifter?) of the jacket got to the sign-in sheet, he picked his jacket up off the floor and signed in with an arrogant and condescending flourish.

"Sit down," I growled, pointing to the chair at the end of the table as I picked up a green collar from the pile of collars on the table. He sat, but, as I turned to flip the collar around his neck, he drew back, put up one hand and said,

"You're not putting that collar on me," as he stood up to look down on me.

"You're right," I said. "I'm not putting this collar on you. He is." And I handed the collar to a large black male facilitator standing beside the chair.

"Here," I said to the black male. "You collar him, please."

"I'll be glad to," said the black male, grinning with delight, and the Bluey stood stock still as the collar encircled his neck. The other participants waiting to be collared and/or sent to the Blue Room were absolutely silent.

"Now, take this boy to the holding room," I told him, and the facilitators and the Bluey were marched away.

I finished registering the group and then went into the meeting room and began preparing the Browns for the exercise. I warned them that we were probably going to have a rocky ride for the morning and told them what had transpired before the registration began. They were a little shocked and a little unbelieving: After all, the behavior I was describing was not that of a mature adult corporation employee. I reminded them that we were not dealing with a mature adult in this boy: he had already been reduced to his child ego state and the chances of his deciding to behave as an adult were very slim, particularly since I had already decided to be in my parent state when dealing with him. He didn't have any more chance of being successful at deterring this exercise than a terrier has of stopping a tornado. One of us knew that for sure.

At the appointed time, the facilitators brought the Blueys

into the room and the fun began immediately. The first thing the 'boy' did was to lead his group in and then gather them around him at the door, saying,

"Don't sit down, yet." I told the Blueys to sit down in their designated place in the middle of the room. Two of them did, but the rest waited for directions from their noble leader. He and a tall over-fiftyish white male continued to stand near the door and began to demand that they be given better chairs and placement within the brown group. I told them again to sit down and to be quiet. Now the blue boy began to point to the signs and say,

"Look at this! This isn't an appropriate learning environment. We demand that you provide us with a proper learning environment." I told them to sit down and follow the rules.

His tall male cohort said, "We don't have to sit where these signs are."

"No," Blue Boy agreed, "let's tear them down." The two of them then commenced to pull the signs off the wall, throw them on the floor and walk on them! The Browns began to discuss these ugly behaviors as being what we can typically expect of Blueys. At this point the blue boy charged around the group, demanding a place to sit until he stopped in front of a Japanese American female sitting on the end of the row on the left side of the room.

"YOU!" he said, pointing his finger in her face, "YOU get up and give me your chair. You sit on the floor. That's where you belong." There was an audible gasp in the room as the members of both groups realized what he had just done. Condemnation by the Browns was immediate and unanimous.

His tall cohort began to look less convinced of the righteousness of the cause to which he'd committed himself as the Japanese American female looked up at the blue boy and, with great dignity and composure, advised the fool to sit down and stop trying to exercise power he didn't have. At that the boy pushed through those Blues who were still standing and made his way to the front of the room where he once again demanded that he be given a proper place to sit. At that point a tall, willowy blue-eyed young woman with long blond hair who had been sitting on one of the chairs in the front row of the Bluey's section, stood, folded her legs and, with extreme grace, simply floated down to sit on the floor. She then half-turned, patted the seat of the chair which she had just vacated, and said,

"There's a place for you to sit. Now, sit down." Seeing that, a number of the blues slid quietly onto chairs in the Bluey's area. But not Blue Boy! He was infuriated!! He charged across the room in front of the group, positioned himself before a Japanese American male and, standing over him, fists on hips, demanded that this brown-eyed male give up his chair. The Japanese American male stood and, nose to nose with Bluey advised him to sit down and let the learning proceed.

He repeatedly said, "Why don't you just sit down and listen?" The boy finally leaned back and, arms folded across his chest, sat on the table in front of me.

I reached over and pushed against the back of his shoulder with my finger, saying as I did so, "Get your butt off the table. This table is not for sitting on." At that the boy whirled around, feet on the floor, eyes wide, trembling and shouting as he reached across the table and slapped me across the upper arm three times as hard as he could from that distance and then, realizing his mistake, began to shout,

"She's hitting me! Don't you hit me! Stop hitting me!"

Amazed and offended, and I must admit, tickled pink, I leaned across the table and with my finger as close to his face as I could get it said quietly, "Now Sucker, I'm going to sue you for assault and battery and I have forty witnesses here to the fact that you just assaulted me. Now what are you going to do?" By this time he was nearly incoherent. He'd gone too far, was out of control and now, had nowhere to go.

Instantly Linda Guillory was in front of him, saying, "Now, you've gone too far! This is not part of the exercise. Get your butt out of this room! NOW!" He tried to protest, but the head of the Human Resources department was standing at the door beckoning to him to get out of the room. His tall associate was already on the way out of the room and every other blue-eye was on a chair or on the floor in the blue-eyed section. Their protest was over.

As the facilitator and the head of the department escorted the two outcasts from the hall, the Browns replaced the signs which had been torn from the walls and we went on with the exercise – after the group had voted not to allow the two loons back into the workshop under any circumstances whatsoever – and had many of the same experiences that the exercise always produces.

When we had completed the exercise and were in the circle ready for our first debriefing, I told the group that the exercise was over, that the blue-eyes were just as good as brown eyes and asked whether there were any questions. A white female raised her hand and said,

"How long did it take you to train those guys to act that way? They are really good actors!"

I nearly lost it at that moment. "Do you mean to tell me that you thought we planned that?" I gasped!

"Well, yes! Didn't you?" she asked. All the facilitators were absolutely appalled.

"Do you mean that was real?" another participant asked.

"Do you want to see my bruises?" I demanded. Then I said, "Do you really think I would take money from your corporation to come out here and let some little piss-ant hit me? That would be another form of prostitution! Yes, their behaviors were real!" I was most angry at the idea that she thought that white males would have to be trained to act as these males had, that white males don't lose control of themselves when they find that they can't control the situation or the people in it. When I asked the group how they would have reacted if two black males had exhibited the behaviors that we had seen that morning, they admitted that their interpretation of the behaviors would probably have been very different.

No, these two men weren't subsequently fired. No, I didn't want them to be. No, I didn't sue them or the corporation. No, I didn't demand an apology. It wasn't until later when I was told that the boy who hit me was a member of the Aryan Nation and told people that, as it was quoted to me, "Elliott's got to go. She's on the top of our list of people to die," that I began to be really disgusted. Did I hear him say it? No. Do I believe he might have said it? Yes. I saw his eyes as he turned on me: He felt cornered and responded as many people who feel cornered would like to respond to unfair treatment. However, if they did, they'd be literally risking their lives. He was risking nothing with his behaviors. That in itself was a large lesson to come from this "harmless little exercise." We all learned a lot during that exercise, but we learned even more, I think, from the woman who indicated that she thought it was all an act!

Article written by employee, Herb Hackenburg and published in the Mountain Bell Times, publication date unknown:

A visit (with some trepidation) with the brown eyes/blue eyes lady

The scene: Four people are riding an elevator down from the 50th floor of Mountain Bell Center. The white, male writer tells his friend, a black, male writer, that it is with some trepidation that he is heading for the Training Center to interview Jane Elliott, the "Brown-eyed, Blue-eyed" lady. While the friend asks, "Who's Jane Elliott?," the two other elevator passengers, whom the white writer had never met, nod knowingly. Then the black writer, a relatively new employee to Mountain Bell, witnesses a phenomenon which may be unique to Mountain Bell employees – his three fellow passengers begin to talk in their own code.

"I didn't enjoy the experience on damn bit, but I remember it like it was yesterday. I still carry my key ring," the blue-eyed lady says. "Oh, I didn't think it was so bad. And I have my key ring, too," the brown-eyed male says with a smile. The blue-eyed writer says, "I've had more enjoyable assignments, but never any more memorable. But what's with the key rings?" Then the elevator door open to the lobby and the passengers depart. The blue-eyed writer tells his perplexed friend he'll explain the next day.

Yes, most of those employees who have attended Mountain Bell's Pluralism Experience Workshop would probably agree that Jane Elliott, the petite, gray-haired, former third grade teacher from Riceville, Iowa, has had a profound effect upon the company's employee force, not as much of an effect as she would like to admit, but an effect nonetheless.

Since 1985, Jane Elliott has been helping to put the "experience" in the Pluralism Experience Workshop by putting workshop attendees through her nationally renowned "brown-eyed, blue-eyed" exercise.

The exercise, which allows participants to experience a few hours of harsh, bigoted treatment based upon the color of their eyes, was originally created by Elliott as a teaching aid for her third-graders.

"It was in 1968, the morning after Martin Luther King was killed, I had no way to tell my kids why he was killed," she explains. "King had been one of our heroes during the month of February, along with George Washington, Abraham Lincoln, Davy Crockett and Daniel

Boone. And there were people who were saying they were glad that he (King) got what was coming to him." Elliott continues, "I vowed that no student would ever leave my classroom with those attitudes intact. So I came up with the brown-eyed, blue-eyed exercise. It helped my kids think about and question bigotry. Now I conduct the exercise with adults."

Jane Elliott and her exercise have been featured on national television, in national magazines and in many of the nation's major newspapers. She has been called thought-provoking, courageous, insulting, a Communist and a Nazi. "And those are the nicer things," she says with a laugh.

Most who have met her would agree that equivocating in not part of Elliott's makeup and there is little doubt where she stands on most issues. Here are some of Elliott's thoughts concerning her work with Mountain Bell's Pluralism Experience Workshop.

Q: It's been said that the people who really need it aren't participating in the Pluralism Workshop. Are the "right" people attending the workshop?

A: I think you are getting the right people for now, but you're not getting the right people for the future. I think more of you craft people who are going to be your future managers should attend the workshop. You're getting your officers, and many of your managers to attend, but you aren't really solving the whole problem. It's your craft people who deal with your customers. And aren't your customers 60 percent minorities and women? Shouldn't your craft people be the ones who are becoming aware of pluralism issues...becoming sensitized?

Q: What do you think about Mountain Bell doing this project?

A: I think that it is amazing! I think that it is amazing that they started it at all, and it's even more amazing that they are still doing it after two years. I know of no other company in the country putting this kind of money and effort into anything similar. I would like to see this lovely, worldwide, 100-year-old corporation tell such a strong story to the rest of the world about not tolerating sexism, racism or ageism. Now US West is sending participants to the workshop and has expressed its commitment to having a pluralistic work force.

Q: Haven't you added ageism to your message?

A: Yes, I've added ageism. You see, some of us won't be adversely affected by sexism and some of us won't be adversely affected by racism, but it's a simple irrefutable fact, that all of us will be adversely affected by ageism. If you live long enough, you will reap what you have sown. If you are lucky enough to get old, you'll find that you're not lucky, unless we change the way we live our lives, raise our children and run our corporations. You cannot go through this exercise and furlough employees at 55, because that is a direct contradiction of the exercise. If you aren't going to live by it (the exercise) as a corporation, don't expect your employees to live by it. Believe me, beyond the ethical and social issues we've been talking about, there is a bottom line issue here.

Q: Would you care to expand on the bottom line issue?

A: You bet. Just what is the fastest growing customer base anyway? By year 2000, 80 percent of those coming into the work force are going to be women and minority group members. They are going to be running our corporations, our governments, our police departments, buying our products and diagnosing and treating our illnesses. They will be helping us to live longer, thus making more of us old people who make up your other fast-growing customer base.

Q: Over the years you've been conducting the exercise you've had many extraordinary experiences. Care to give an example or two?

A: Indeed. My life was threatened in Pennsylvania when I conducted a short two-hour form of the exercise to a group of 400 teachers. I ended up having to escorted out of town by an armed guard. And I've had college faculty members lead a class revolt. Here at Mountain Bell, I had a female disrupt the class to the point where I had to call the security guards to escort her out of the room. She did come back and began to take advantage of the learning experience. In another experience, the class was deliberately disrupted by two men who, from what they said and by their actions, were either members of or sympathizers of the Aryan Nation organization. And I've had some blue-eyed people come to the exercise wearing brown contact lenses. Overall, however, the exercises I've conducted at Mountain Bell have been productive learning experiences.

Q: How does a white male express concern about early signs of individuals within employee support groups, which were founded and continue to function for excellent and logical reasons, beginning to pursue their own individual agendas thereby detracting from the corporation's agenda, without coming off as a pompous, sexist, racist?

A: I don't know. If the white males in power are as smart as they think they are, they should be able to convey the idea that the survival of the company many times depends on everyone's individual interests becoming less important than the good of the whole. If Mountain Bell is going to survive, that's a problem we're all going to have to work on together. The phone company is getting into an extremely competitive environment and doesn't need any extra problems. I know today's white males have been asked to give a whole lot, so special interest groups are going to have to give some, too. But let's not forget that members of these groups have been giving for a lot of years.

Q: What's the significance of the key ring?

A: I wanted those who had fortitude enough to go through the exercise to have a memento of the experience. As you now, the blue-eyed people in the class have to wear a little green collar, so my daughter and I designed a key ring with a little green collar on it. Hopefully, the key ring will remind them of what they learned in the exercise.

Q: If you could say just one thing to MB Times readers, what would it be?

A: I'd tell them that they, and they alone, are responsible for their own racism, their own sexism, their own ageism. They cannot blame their parents, their religious upbringing, or their community for their behavior. As adults they are responsible for the attitudes they have, the things they do, and the things they say. As adults we have demanded responsibility, so we should be held accountable for our actions be they negative or positive.

18 A Remarkable Lesson From a Viet Nam Vet

The most memorable exercise that I ever conducted took place in the Doubletree Hotel in Aurora, Colorado. The facilitators and I had prepared the room as usual – put up the signs, arranged the chairs, put the pencils and paper pads on the chairs for the Browns and set up the registration table in the hall. The hotel caterers had delivered the snacks as usual and we were ready to go. I came out of the meeting room to find the approximately 40 adult corporate employees lounging about in the area outside the room. The men were doing what many (not all) men in workplace situations do; standing around rocking back and forth from their heels to their toes with their hands deep in the front pockets of their pants, their fingers busily manipulating their valuables. Many of the women were either standing or sitting around gazing up at the men with that Nancy Reagan "Oh-you-wonderful-thing-you" look.

I stood by the registration table and announced, "You people get over here and sign in."

One of the tall, fairly young men turned to look at me, then turned back to the group which he'd been gracing with his presence and said loudly, "Sounds like she got up on the wrong side of the bed this morning." Outwardly I ignored the comment. Inwardly, I began to cheer.

I said, a little more loudly and with a little more emphasis, "Get over here and sign in NOW!" The tall one sauntered over, leading the chattering, laughing group to the table. As they lined-up behind him, he leaned over the table, placed one hand on each side of the sign-in pad, read the heading of the page and then, still bent over, turned his head to look up at me and said, "What color ARE my eyes?"

"Don't you know what color your eyes are, Sonny?" I asked, more curtly than was necessary.

"No," he sneered. "You tell me."

"Do you have a drivers license?" I asked him. At this point, he straightened up to his full height and said loudly,

"Of course!"

"Well, take it out and take it over there and show it to someone so they can read it to you so you'll know what color your eyes are." I snapped.

At that, he wheeled away from me and, as he strode down the line of waiting victims, he announced, "She's a real bitch!" All laughing and chattering stopped as his peers waited, some I think in trepidation and some in anticipation, for my reaction to his statement. Outwardly I ignored it because, you see, I was fully aware that his treatment was supposed to intimidate me, and if his body language and his behavior didn't get the job done, the word 'bitch' was supposed to reduce me to an apologetic state if not to tears. He was unaware that for me that word is an acronym for "Being in Total Control Honey". I was, and he wasn't. His problem was that I knew that and he didn't.

As he stomped away and I went on registering the rest of the participants I was thinking, "Oh, my tall young friend, your ass is grass and I'm about to mow it. You will be a Bluey today if it's the last thing I ever do." Little did I know that he was thinking about the last thing I'd ever do, too.

When I'd finished registering the group and all the participants had been sent to their assigned rooms, I went into the meeting room and prepared the Browns for the day. We all knew that one of the Blues was going to be a problem and most of the Browns seemed a little concerned. Did they know something I didn't? Did they EVER!

When we'd done the listening skills and the culturally biased test, and had discussed our individual responsibility for creating an effective learning experience for the Blues, we sent one of the facilitators to escort them to the meeting room. As I expected, the resentful one led the pack into the room and ushered the females to the chairs. His actions were courtly, but dumb (Blueys don't plan ahead.). Then, since there were no more chairs in the center of the room he asked where he was expected to sit. I indicated that he should sit on the floor. He sat down on the floor behind the last 2 chairs (Blueys don't consider the consequences of their behaviors before they act.). Of course, I reprimanded him because he wasn't going to be able to see from there or to practice the physical aspects of the listening skills (Blues don't care about paying attention; they don't come to learn, anyway). He got up and walked over to sit on one of the chairs in the Brown section (Blueys won't stay in their place; they always want to be where they aren't wanted). The Browns refused to let the Bluey sit in their section (they were fully aware that if you let in one of those people they'll ruin the neighborhood.). Now the increasingly disgusted Bluey demanded a chair…to no avail. He refused to sit on the floor at the front of the room. I told him that he'd either sit on the floor or get out the door.

"It's my way or the highway," I said (you have to speak in the kind of language Blueys are most likely to understand). It took us about 10 minutes to get the obstinate one on the floor. The minute he sat down I announced that the Blues were to take all their junk and put it under the table at the back of the room. (you never know what they might be carrying in their briefcases). All the Blues took all their purses, briefcases, notebooks, etc. and put them under the table as directed. Then, since they weren't paying attention after they sat back down but were reading the signs on the walls, (the signs had large, colorful, cartoon-like characters on them and blues are notoriously distractible), I had them read the signs individually. When it was the angry one's turn to read he stood and loudly read,

"Why can't 'ay' Blue-eye be more like 'ay' Brown?"

"That's wrong," I said. "Read it again and get it right." He gritted his teeth, glared down at me and said, louder and with emphasis,

"Why can't AY Blue-eye be more like AY Brown?"

"That's wrong. Do it over and get it right," I commanded again. Same response, but this time with a sarcastic and condescending expression designed to let me know that he was only allowing me to get away with this (he had developed a definite attitude, which is what his people are likely to do when challenged).

"Sit down," I told him, and pointing to the blue-eyed female beside him, I said, "You read it. I'll bet you can get it right." She stood and read,

"Why can't a Blue-eye be more like a Brown?" No problem. Well, everyone knows that women are generally more likely to do language-related things right the first time. They have a greater facility for language than men do, for the most part, and they are conditioned to avoid making mistakes because their errors will be blamed on their gender, more often than not. The Browns and I discussed the 'fact' as the Blues stewed. When all the signs had been read, I asked each of the Blues whether they knew the listening skills. Since the angry one was on the floor in the front of the group, he was one of the first to be asked. Did he know the physical aspects of the listening skills? Of course he did. What were they? Maintain eye contact with the speaker. Then what can all the other group members do while he and the speaker are maintaining eye contact: go out for coffee? How often must the speaker repeat her-or himself- in a room of thirty-five people if that's one of the listening skills? Makes no sense to me. Bad answer. The rest of the Blues admitted upon being questioned that they'd been about to offer same wrong response (you know how they are; they are all alike). So now I was forced to teach them skills which they should have learned in grammar school.

"Take out a piece of paper and a pencil," I directed. Up the Blueys jumped and headed for the table at the back of the room. "Hey! Where are you going? Sit down!" I commanded. Down they sat. "Where's your paper and pencil?" I asked the first Bluey beside me.

"In my purse," she replied.

"Why don't you have it with you?" I asked.

"You told me to put it under that table," she answered.

"Did I tell them to put their paper and pencils under that

table?" I asked the Browns.

"No!" they chorused.

"What did I tell them to put under that table?" I prompted.

"Their junk!" they sang.

"What do Blues think learning materials are?" I chanted.

"Junk!" the Browns sang out. The rhythm was now established, and it was now obvious who was to be the director and who the chorus – and who didn't know the words. Shaking my head in mock despair at their inadequacies, I began to hand out paper and pencils to the Blueys (You know how they are, they're never prepared. And no matter how much you give them they're never satisfied: they always want more and more). Did they say 'thank you' for the materials I provided for them? Of course not (Blueys are ungrateful. And some of them had developed an attitude). When everyone finally seemed ready to begin I told them that they were to write exactly what I said exactly as I said it. They were to use no contractions, no abbreviations, no shorthand, no symbols other than letters and numbers. Did they understand? Of course they said they did.

I said, "Number one," and recited the first listening skill. The belligerent one wrote 'Number 1' on his paper. I watched. I waited. I asked him,

"Do you know what a redundancy is?"

"You said to write exactly what you said," he retorted (Blueys are very literal thinkers – when they think at all – but this boy was really just being cute).

"Stop playing, 'Trick the Teacher' and get the job done right," I scolded. He put the '1' on his paper and tried to write the first listening skill. He'd forgotten it. I repeated it, "

"Good listeners have quiet hands, feet, and mouths." He wrote it. I watched. I waited.

Then I asked him asked him,

"How do you spell 'quiet'?" As if I didn't know. He said,

"Q-u-i-t-e."

"Well, that's quite good, but it's not quite 'quiet', is it?" I asked.

He replied, "It is, as far as I'm concerned."

Well, it wasn't good enough for me so I said, "Do it over and get it right."

He tried "Q-u-e-i-t."

Nope. "Sound it out. What's the first sound in quiet?" I asked.

"Kwuh," he answered.

"And what letters stand for that sound 'kwuh' in quiet?" I asked.

"Q-u," he ground out.

"Write it." He wrote. We proceeded through the rest of the word. Then I had him spell the word out loud as he wrote it five times. Was I doing this to be mean to him? No. And the Browns all agreed that I was doing it for his (Let's say it all together...)

"Own good."

"How should he feel about my taking extra time and energy to teach him something he should have learned years ago?"

The Browns caroled, "GRATEFUL!" On the second listening skill he had trouble with 'their' and his penmanship had begun to deteriorate. On the third skill I waited until all the Blueys had finished writing and then asked them,

"How many 'n's do you have in the word 'beginning'?"

Half of the group, including the Blue Boy, said, "Two!"

The other half said, "Three!"

"Look, Bluey," I said. "Spell the word, 'beginning' out loud and count the 'n's, as you say them." He snarled,

"B-e-g-i-n-n-i-n-g. Two!" Browns began to grin.

I said, "Look at your paper. Put your finger on each of the letters as you say them and count the 'n's out loud."

He pointed at each letter as he said, "B-e-g-i-n-n-i-n-g, two!" Now the browns were audibly chuckling.

"All right," I said. "We're going to do this one more time. This time, point to the letters with the first finger of your right hand and when you see an 'n' raise one finger of your left hand. Do it." He began,

"B-e-g-i-n- (up went one finger) n-(up went another finger) i-n- (up slowly, went another finger) g...three."

"Now, how may 'n's are there in 'beginning'?" I badgered. At this he threw his paper and pencil down, unpinned his collar, stood up, deposited the pin and the collar on my head with decisive force and stormed from the room. One of the facilitators followed him into the hall. As those of us left in the room discussed his behavior as being typical of what you can expect of "those people", the facilitator informed him that he was free to leave the workshop, but that his failure to complete the three day course would be part of his personnel file and might affect his future raises and promotions. He came back into the room. (That's called "mo-ti-va-tion".)

As he moved to resume his position at the front of the room, I stopped him in the middle of the aisle and said, "You won't be allowed back into this room until you have apologized to every female and every person of color in this room. You have just exercised a freedom that a whole lot of us don't have: When you got tired of being treated negatively on the basis of your eye color, you could just walk out and not be subjected to that unfairness anymore. When females get tired of sexism they can't just walk away; there's no place in this society that is free of sexism. And when people of color get tired of racism in this society they can't just walk away because wherever they go they'll continue to encounter racism. Racist conditioning has been a part of this society ever since the white people got here, and it is everywhere. Now what are you going to do?"

It took about seven minutes to get him to admit that the mistake was his and to get him back in his place. We went on with the lesson. When the exercise was over, we took a short break as I put the chairs in a circle. Then we sat down, Blues and Browns side by side and I said, "The exercise is over. Blue-eyed people are just as good as Brown-eyed people. Does anyone have anything they want to say?"

The angry young man was sitting directly across from me and he immediately raised his hand and said, "There's something I want to say, Mrs. Elliott."

161

"What is it?" I asked, prepared for the worst, but not expecting what I got.

"You came this close to dying today," he said, as he raised his right hand, holding this thumb and forefinger about a quarter of an inch apart. The rest of the group started to laugh. I didn't laugh; I was looking into his eyes.

"You're absolutely serious, aren't you?" I asked.

"Yes," he said. "You'll never come that close to death again without dying. I could see myself putting you through that wall behind you with one blow. I could have broken every bone in your body with two blows; I was trained to do that as a Navy SEAL during the Viet Nam War." He went on to say, "I've never been as mad at anyone as I was at you today, except for one time. I went through Navy SEAL training with a black buddy. It was our job to keep one another alive. They put us through the training and sent us to Viet Nam. We were in a firefight and my black buddy was wounded and he was out in the middle of a field screaming for me to help him and my superior officer wouldn't let me go and I wanted to kill him that day the way I wanted to kill you today."

"And when you got home we called you a 'baby killer', didn't we?" I asked.

"Yeah," he responded.

"And when they brought you home, did they tell you to change into your civilian clothes before you got off the plane?" I asked.

"Yeah, they told us people would spit on us in the airport if we didn't," he said. Then he went on, "When our plane landed in the states I went to the airport and dialed my mom's number with the blood and the mud from Viet Nam still under my fingernails. I told her I was in the States and she said, 'Don't come home now; feelings are too high here. Go to your grandmother's house and stay for a month. If you come home now something awful will happen.'" He paused and took a deep breath, and leaning forward with his elbows on his knees he looked at me and said, "I want to thank you for what you did here, today. This is the first time I've been in a group where I felt secure enough to talk about any of this. I haven't even shared any of this with my family." We were all simply devastated. What have we done?

We finished that debriefing - and a very subdued debriefing it was - and then went to lunch. After lunch, as I was sitting alone at a table getting ready to leave for the airport, that remarkable man came to my table and, standing over me, said,

"Mrs. Elliott, may I ask a favor of you?"

"Sure," I said, "what is it?"

"May I hug you?" he asked. I'm sorry to say it, but my first thought was, he "could break every bone in my body with two blows!" My second thought was, "This is called 'risk taking'. You put yourself out there; now live with the consequences of your behavior."

"Sure," I said, as I stood up. "I think that would be fine."

That tall, strong young man bent to put his arms around me and, while holding me tightly, said, "I want to thank you again for what you did today. You gave me back my life. I had put my life on hold when I came back from Nam. Now, I can start to live again."

How many Viet Nam veterans have put their lives on hold

until the rest of us get over the guilt we feel about Viet Nam? How long will we retain the stereotypes we have of those veterans and treat them like second-class citizens just because this country has decided it made a mistake? We didn't stereotype those in the government who let (made?) that happen; we've only stereotyped the young men we sent to do that dirty job. Robert McNamara admitted his mistake; when will the rest of us admit ours?

I will never forget that young man and what he taught me and the rest of the people in that room, that day. And I'll never listen quietly to someone trying to justify sending young men and women into harm's way and forcing them to fight another old men's war.

19 Winning With Winfrey

In the summer of 1986 a member of Oprah Winfrey's staff called me and asked me if I'd do the Blue-eyed, Brown-eyed exercise live on her daytime talk show. I'd never heard of Oprah Winfrey, since she hadn't gone national yet, but, since I'd done several television news and talk shows by then (Tonight Show, Donahue, Virginia Graham, Today, etc.), I wasn't nervous about being in front of cameras. And, since I'd done the exercise with numerous groups of adults by then, I wasn't nervous about my ability to deal with the participants and their reactions to the exercise. However, I wasn't comfortable with dealing with confrontations with adults live on camera. I consoled myself with the idea that it was only a local show and how many people in Chicago would see me after the show was aired? That worked and, happily self-hypnotized, I went to Chicago and put Oprah's audience through the exercise. It was terrific!! For me. Because it worked. People got angry. They got confused. Some became withdrawn. Some understood. Some didn't understand. Some said it was unfair. Some enjoyed it. Oprah helped. Many learned. I was pleased and when, that fall, after she went national, they called and asked me to repeat the exercise with another group, I consented to do so.

The second time we did the Oprah show both the studio and the audience were larger, the atmosphere was more formal, and I felt a bit like one of Her Majesty's minions. I wasn't particularly pleased with the environment, and when Oprah put her arm around a blue-eyed person's shoulders to comfort her during the exercise, I was downright pissed! That one act effectively destroyed the reality of the exercise for that group. I realized, after thinking it over, that Oprah had probably been cautioned by her associates to treat the white folks with care during the exercise, if she didn't want to lose her sponsors, so she was only doing what she had to. However, even though I thought I understood the situation, I found it hard to accept.

We had several hours to wait before our flight home after the show so, after we'd shopped a bit, we went to the Midway airport snack bar to have a bite to eat. We sat down at a table in the snack area and a young woman came to take our order. She glanced around our table, counting noses, pencil poised to write until... her eyes landed on me. Instantly she put her hand out toward me as if to ward off a blow, took three rapid steps backward and said in great agitation, "Don't look at me! I'm not waiting on you! I've got blue eyes!" Then she turned and almost ran away! We were simply stunned. Sarah and her husband, Abdulwahab Salamah, were with Darald and me and we all began to react at once.

"She saw the Oprah show!"

"She believed it!"

"She's really upset!!!"

"Maybe we'd better go hide out somewhere!"

"Do you think they'll wait on us here?" Up until that moment Wahab had been quietly skeptical about my descriptions of how adults react to being in the exercise. That exercise really altered his attitude toward the whole thing.

Another young woman came over and took our order, but,

the distraught one hung around in the background, almost, it seemed, fascinated by being this close to what she obviously perceived as a malevolent live-right-on-earth monster.

In the spring of 1994 Oprah was planning on doing a show on racism in parents as part of her yearlong once-a-month discussion of racism. I admired her for taking on this issue and when one of her assistant producers called me and asked if I'd be a panel member on the show I was happy to oblige. I thought the show was going to be a discussion of what parents can do to avoid raising racist children so I jumped at the chance to appear.

Upon our arrival at the Harpo studios that morning we were taken to the "green room" where we met the other panel members for that morning's taping and where I was to wait to have my makeup done. I discovered, while visiting with those in the room, that three of them were parents whose offspring had disgraced their families by dating people 'outside' their race, as one of the fathers so disgustingly put it. As I visited with them and listened to their discussion of 'the problem' I understood what they were saying and why they were saying it and who they were and where these statements were originating, but I didn't understand how they felt so free to make those statements to a stranger. Was it because I was white and they assumed that we were of the same mind? How did they dare make those remarks in the presence of the Black man who was doing our makeup? Were they only being ignorant and insensitive or was it a deliberate insult? One of the women participants indicated very curtly to the room at large that she didn't' need his makeup; she'd done her own. And had she ever! I didn't understand why she was so adamant about not needing to have help with her makeup until I watched her during the show, as she told Oprah that her mother had told her never to let a Black man lay a hand on her. And, as it happened, it was a good thing that she had taken her mother's advice on this day, because it took a considerable amount of time to get my face ready for the camera.

After my makeover, Christine Tardio, Oprah's executive producer (I think) came to get me and took me into a small room to watch the first part of the show and to discuss what she wanted me to do on the show. Before she got a chance to inform me of her plans, I pointed to the father who by now was sitting on the platform in the studio and said, "I'm going after that father."

She didn't ask me why I'd do such a thing. She simply commenced to tell me about an incident which the man's daughter had shared with Oprah's people in which the man had deliberately set the girl and her boyfriend up by inviting them to a family dinner in a prestigious restaurant and then proceeded to beat her in front of the rest of the patrons in order to teach her what the consequences were if she continued to date her Hispanic boyfriend. She then shared with me some of the racist statements that had been made by the show's guests on the previous day's taping. Those same old racist statements that white folks use who think they're being rational and reasonable and aren't supposed to cause umbrage in anyone. Things like:

"You people are always looking for racism. If you'd quit looking for it you wouldn't be finding it all the time," and,

"Why can't you all just relax?" and

"White males are the ones who are being discriminated against in this country today," and

"Why don't you all stop acting like victims?"

I wasn't surprised at the statements and I asked, "Did Oprah say, 'You can't find racism if it isn't there,' and, 'We'd love to relax and if you'll just stop arresting and imprisoning and hassling and refusing to educate our young men, we'll be more than happy to,' and, 'You need to look at the statistics before you start making these irresponsible statements,' and, 'You've got the cart before the horse, here; When you stop victimizing people they'll stop acting like victims!'?"

"Jane," Chris said, "Oprah's a black female hosting the show. She can't say those things. It will look like she's pushing her own agenda. But you can say them." She had been sketching the plans for the remaining three fourths of the show on a chart pad and had written me in for the last half. At this point she took her magic marker and drew a large arrow up from my name in the middle of the chart to the end of the first quarter of the show and said, "We're putting you in here. Say whatever you have to."

"Now wait," I said. "How much control is Oprah willing to give up on this?"

"Don't worry about that," Chris said. "Oprah wants this to happen. You go to it."

By the time the first 15 minutes of the show had been taped, she'd gotten the Mercator Projection map and the Peters Projection map mounted on a large easel and had informed Oprah as to what was to take place. The stagehands (technicians?) seated me on the stage between the swaggering (even while sitting down) father and the did-my-own-makeup mother and, after the commercial break, Oprah introduced me to the audience. She then asked me to describe what I do and I said, as I remember, "I do an exercise in discrimination in which I separate groups according to their eye color and discriminate against those who have the wrong color eyes. And that," I said, turning to Mr. Perfect, "is what's wrong with you. If you didn't have those green eyes, you wouldn't be such a fool." He gasped, drew back as if to avoid being punched and blurted,

"Hey! What's wrong with me?"

I commenced to tell him. The audience members were shocked but delighted. Even though they didn't know why I was so viciously attacking him they obviously sensed that I knew something about him that they hadn't been told. I did and I was utterly disgusted with him, his previous treatment of his daughter because of her dating an Hispanic male, and the repulsive and repugnant remarks he'd made in the green room and on the first segment of the show. I was almost as disgusted with his daughter because the moment I confronted him she began to defend his philosophy and his behaviors, even though she and I both knew that if what she'd told Tardio before we came on the show was true, his actions were absolutely indefensible.

It was an interesting show and, when it was over, many members of the audience asked Oprah if they could "do the exercise". She said,

"Sure. We can do that this afternoon for next month's show, can't we?" to Christine Tardio and they began to make plans. I was standing a little distance from her when I heard that remark. I stepped up and said,

"Wait a minute, Oprah. Did you say we could do that today?"

"Sure," she answered. "Why not?"

"Well, we need collars," I began.

"Well, you can cut those, can't you?" she asked with some impatience.

"I could if I wanted to," I answered. "But you don't

understand. These folks all know now what's going to happen. You've already lost the element of surprise. Furthermore, these are folks who want to do the exercise. That in itself destroys the reality. Most people of color and women don't volunteer for the abuse. Besides, I'm busy this afternoon."

"What are you doing this afternoon?" she demanded.

"Well, I'm going home," I laughed.

"Then when can you do it?" she asked.

"What are you doing two weeks from today?" I asked. "I can do it then."

"Can we schedule it for then?" Oprah asked one of the employees standing beside her. After some checking it was decided that they would contact me later to firm up the date and I returned to the green room to remove my makeup, gather up my belongings, and leave for the airport. Security people escorted us out of the studio to a waiting limousine as the angry male parent and his daughter and their companions stood by, glaring. I was grateful for the security people.

Two weeks later I flew back to Chicago, collars and courage in-hand, prepared to do the exercise, I thought. This time, instead of the audience members being confined in a small space inside the building, they were milling around in the lobby and outside in the street. They had been told to come to the studio early deliberately so that they would be tired of standing around waiting before they met me. Accompanied by 2 men carrying cameras, I walked into that group, indicating to the brown-eyed individuals that they were to go upstairs with the show's escorts, and handing collars to the non-browns, saying, "Pin this around your neck and don't lose it. And try to keep the noise down out here." No please or thank you or explanation. The reactions were immediate. Some tried to argue. Some tried to protest. Some tried to refuse to comply. One tall young man said,

"And what if I don't wear it?"

"And what if we put you out of the building?" I responded. He and the older females standing around him looked at one another, shrugged, laughed nervously and then, in concert, put their collars on. Several people left the studio rather than comply with my demands. That was fine; there were too many non-browns, anyway.

After the non-browns had been collared, I went upstairs to where the browns were being served coffee and doughnuts and began conditioning them for what was coming. As usual, the people of color were surprised and delighted and as usual the whites were surprised and confused and as usual one brown-eyed white woman said she and her friend could not agree with this and would not go along.

"Fine," I said. "Then you're outta' here. Go be a Bluey."

"Is that my only choice?" she asked.

"Sure is," I told her. She got up off the floor where she'd been sitting and motioned to her friend to join her as she left. The friend sat still.

"Aren't you going with your friend?" I asked her.

"She doesn't speak for me," the woman said, and watched as the pages led her friend from the area.

"Wait a minute," I said to the page as they reached the top of the stairs. "Don't put her in with the non-browns. She'll contaminate the group. Put her on a chair in the hall where you can watch her." I turned back to look at her companion, thinking that by now she'd had time to think about what she was doing and would have changed her mind. She saw me looking at her and dropped her eyes to her hands. "How did you get here today?" I asked her. "In a car?"

"Yeah," she muttered.

"With her?" I asked, jerking my head in the direction of the ejected one's back.

"Yes," she replied a trifle more defiantly.

"And are you planning on riding home in the same car with her?" I wondered.

"Should be an interesting trip…" someone in the group said. There was a murmur of assent from the rest of the participants, but the 'friend' said not a word – and maintained her seat on the floor.

I finished preparing the group and got their commitment to cooperate with the exercise and then we all headed down the stairs and into the studio. As we walked through the halls we passed the roped-off area in which the non-browns were confined. Hoots, catcalls, and Bronx cheers came from the non-browns. Smug smiles, nudges, and high fives were exchanged among the browns. We took the browns into the studio and seated them on risers on each side of the stage, facing the center section of risers which had been left vacant for the non-browns.

After all the browns were comfortably seated, the pages led the non-browns in. These did not appear to be the same people we had met a short forty to fifty minutes before. Not only were the majority of them wearing ugly green collars, they were now wearing unpleasant, crabby expressions and making angry, disgusting noises and saying pouty petulant things. The browns immediately began to comment on the inferior behaviors and attitudes being exhibited by these malcontents. Several of them were carrying their collars. It was obvious that they weren't going to conform, so very shortly our treatment of them resulted in their storming out of the studio, saying, "We don't have to put up with this shit."

The exercise went as usual. The blues acted as blues always do, the browns did their job with joy and delight and the learning in some of the participants was obvious. So was the anger. At one point a young man dressed in a dark suit and shirt and tie and carrying a briefcase stood and told us, "What happens between the races and the sexes on this earth is not racism and sexism. Someone has to take charge or there would be chaos. It was foreordained that society would be so arranged. It has always been so."

"Oh," I said, "and because you have the proper urinary tract and skin color you are better qualified to take charge than those who are different from yourself?" The women and people of color in the audience hooted derisively.

Oprah said. "Perhaps you should sit down. I'm going to let you rest after that statement." Sit down, he did, but rest, he didn't.

A number of people left that show absolutely furious, frustrated, puzzled, and full of resentment. Even after Oprah apologized to them for what we'd put them through. Even after we'd explained that it was an exercise…that it wasn't real, that it was temporary, that I didn't really feel that way about blue-eyed people. I was amazed, once again, at the inability of some white folks to cope for an hour with a tiny taste of what people of color live with every day in this country. The most oft-repeated complaint during the exercise that day was that I didn't' treat them as individuals, that I made broad generalizations about them, that I didn't know anything about them and so had no business judging them and "tarring them all with the same brush". People of color stood up repeatedly and reminded them that this a daily experience for people of color. What about how they feel? The white folks, in many cases, considered this irrelevant.

In November of that year Oprah invited members of the parent panel and some of those who went through the exercise to come back to her show and share their impressions of their experience with her audience. The green-eyed father was one of those who came back. She asked him whether his experience on the earlier show had changed his attitude at all toward people of color and he said he thought it had. She asked his daughter whether she thought her father had changed and the daughter said she didn't think he had, but she'd never met his new female friend. Oprah then asked her if she'd like to meet the woman and, when the daughter indicated that she would, Oprah told the woman to come on out. And out came an Hispanic female, to the shock of the daughter and delight of the audience. When I heard about the man, and his seeming change of heart, I was not delighted . This man had beaten his daughter for dating "out of her race" with an Hispanic male! Did I believe his conversion? Hell, no! I think if he was dating an Hispanic woman, he was doing it to get even. I was disgusted. I hope I'm wrong, but I doubt that I am. I hope Oprah wasn't set-up. I hope even more fervently that the Hispanic female wasn't set-up.

20 Meeting Some Remarkable Muslims

You may have noticed in the previous passage that our son-in-law doesn't have an Anglo-sounding name. You're right. In 1985 our daughter Sarah was working in Fort Worth, Texas, and met and fell in love with Abdulwahab Mohammed Salamah, a Saudi Arabian who worked for the Arabian American oil company (now SaudiAramco) and was in this country taking business training at TCU in Ft. Worth. They decided that they were going to be married, but first he had to go back to Saudi Arabia and make the arrangements to get her into his country. When he left the USA that spring, he told her to go home and live with her parents! She was not to get a job unless it was working for her father, who owned a Sears catalog store at that time. He would come back for her the following spring. I was incensed! Not because she came to live with us. Not because she couldn't work using her teacher training. Not because she was in love with a Saudi Arab. I was incensed because she was willing to put her life on hold for nearly a year on the word of a man about whom we knew virtually nothing.

So home she came, and what hell we put her through. She called Wahab or he called her several times a week. She cried. He cried. His parents were giving him even more hell than we were giving her. Naturally we thought that was terribly unfair of them; after all, look what a prize he would be getting in our daughter! We warned her repeatedly that he'd never come back for her, that his mother had already arranged a marriage for him just as she had for his older and younger brothers and that she was being foolish.

I made plans for Darald and me to take a tour of the British Isles in May, but he couldn't (wouldn't) get away so I asked Sarah if she'd like to go along. I thought it would take her mind off Wahab and would cheer her up a bit. She cried all over England, Ireland and Wales. While we were in England, Sarah ate something she shouldn't have and was stricken with a severe case of food poisoning. She stopped crying and started vomiting. It just happened that we were at Stonehenge during the summer solstice and all these free spirits and unclad believers were soaring all over the place. The Midwesterners on our tour bus were absolutely scandalized – and fascinated!

"Just look," one of the men said, pointing toward the bushes next to the fence. "There's one of them vomiting in the bushes. Probably drank too much or got too many drugs." I looked over at the bushes and there, indeed, was a young woman in cut-off denim shorts and a tee shirt, bending over and throwing up on the ground.

"That, my friend, is my daughter," I said to the man, "and she's reacting to the bad food which we were served last night, not to drugs or alcohol." He scurried for the bus and I gathered Sarah up and we got back on board. Two days later, when it was Sarah's and my turn to ride in the back seats of the bus (we rotated every day) we both were sick from the ice cream which they'd served us in one of the hotels. Did you ever ride in the back seat of a tour bus in the heat with no lavatory and a bus driver who wants to get to his home town in Wales in a hurry so that he can have a night with his girlfriend, so makes very infrequent and very short stops? Did Darald make a good choice in deciding not to make the trip?

After we returned home, Sarah went back to work at Darald's store and back to calling Wahab and waiting for his calls. We advised her to apply for a teaching position. She refused. Wahab wanted her to stay at home with us. God, that woman is stubborn! We finally simply gave up on that and resigned ourselves to waiting to see what spring would bring. We were steeling ourselves for the explosion there would be in the spring when we were sure Wahab would call to inform her that he'd changed his mind. And sure enough, on a frigid day in January he called – and said to meet him in Rochester, MN. He was on his way to get her and take her back to Saudi Arabia. His uncle had agreed to let her stay at his house on Bahrain until her papers could be approved and then she'd move in with his parents until they could find housing on the ARAMCO compound in Dhahran. Sarah quit crying and I nearly started. Saudi Arabia?? Black clothes!! Oppressed women??? Islam!!! Bedouins!!! Oppressed women!!! Tents! Sand! Men in white dresses! Oppressed women! We'd never met this man.

Sarah flew out of the house and headed for Rochester and Darald and I prepared to meet this Arab who was going to spirit away our daughter. And the next day, here they both came, grinning and shining and totally consumed by one another. I remembered then, how I'd felt about Darald and how determined I was to marry him even though my parents didn't approve. I was so grateful that these two young people seemed to have found what Darald and I did, in spite of all the obstacles we'd placed in their path.

They were married a few days later in the mosque in Cedar Rapids, IA. And then Darald and I took them back to Rochester and put them on a plane for Saudi Arabia! I'd read several books about the Arabs while Sarah was dating Wahab and I was more than a little concerned. So were they, but they were in love and, of course, thought that would make up for all the difficulties. And so far, it seems to have done just that, for they now have two lovely daughters and Darald and I have visited them and Wahab's parents in Saudi Arabia several times. However, I will never forget the feeling I had as I watched that Northwest jet climb into the sky and take our firstborn child to live beside the Persian Gulf.

Distressed as we were at Sarah's decision to marry into a culture so different from the one in which she was raised, I will be eternally grateful for all the things our family has learned as a result of that decision and our getting to know Wahab and his family and his culture. Fortunately for us, his father had been with ARAMCO since the company was first formed and he had traveled extensively in this country – and many others. So, while he and his wife didn't like Wahab's decision to marry an American female, they understood what he was going through and were willing to accept Sarah eventually as someone who was very important to their son. And now, their son has become very important to us, as we enjoy our two half-Saudi, half-American granddaughters.

21 BE/BE Goes International

In the summer of 1994 a film maker from Germany, Bertram VerHoeg, contacted me and asked me if I'd allow him to interview me for a film he was making for German television and which was to deal with subject of prejudice and its roots. Of course I would, so he came and interviewed me in our living room one afternoon. He seemed to be very moved by my responses to his questions and my description of the effects of the blue-eyed, brown-eyed exercise and what I'd learned while doing it. He asked me whether I'd be willing to be the subject of a documentary on German TV. Thinking it would never happen, I consented to do so and he took his camera and crews and went back to Germany. I thought that was the end of that, but he called me frequently during the following year to inform me of the progress he'd made in acquiring funding for this project. I still doubted that the documentary would ever be done, but in the spring of 1995, he called to tell me that he'd arranged the funding, and they'd be there in August to film me doing the blue-eyed, brown-eyed exercise with as many groups as possible. He also wanted footage of me doing a college or university lecture.

As it happened, a large Midwestern fire department not too far from Osage was under a court decree to have me come in and work with their firefighters as part of the settlement of a racial discrimination suit which had been brought against the department by a number of black firefighters. Their fire chief agreed to allow Denkmal, VerHoeg's film company, to film those sessions. I had also been contacted by a Kansas City, Missouri group called "Harmony" which had been formed for the purpose of increasing racial awareness and understanding in the Kansas City area. They had asked me to do some workshops with their group but were having difficulty getting the funding to bring me in. I told them about Ver Hoeg's request that I find some groups with whom we could make a film, and after a number of discussions with Shirley Phoenix, Michelle Campbell, and Mark Rivas, we planned to do two exercises with groups of K.C. volunteers. Ver Hoeg and his crew returned to the USA, and with the help of two marvelous US West Direct facilitators, Cookie Serenpa and Collin Sprisebach, I put the fireones (a nearly totally resistant and resentful group) through the exercise. In the following days, Denkmal filmed as I gave lectures to three large groups of angry fireones (we use 'someone' and 'everyone,' and 'anyone' to describe people, so why can't we do the same with professions and educational levels?) in that same Midwestern city: as I addressed a group of college freshones in Chapman University in Orange County, CA in a program organized by Bonnie Ash; and as I discussed the exercise and what it meant to her adolescence, with my daughter Mary, in her home in Murrieta, CA; and then in Kansas City where we filmed two exercises with the citizen volunteers. We then returned to our home near Osage, where he spent several hours doing interviews in and around our home and the community.

Everything went so smoothly during the interviews that we invited the members of the film crew to stay at our house for dinner after the interviews were over and before they returned to Germany. We were going to have a low- country shrimp boil, which is a meal that's delicious to eat and easy to prepare. I thought. Here's how it works – when it works:

Wash and rinse 6#s of raw shrimp in their shells. Wash 12 to 14 small new red potatoes. Break 16 ears of sweet corn in half. Cut 5#s of smoked sausage links or sweet Italian sausage into 2-3" lengths. Fill one 8-10qt pot half full of water. Add ½ cup butter and 3 tablespoons of salt to water and bring to a boil. Add Tabasco to taste. Put potatoes in water and boil 10 minutes. Put corn in water (w/taters) and boil 5 minutes. Add sausage to water and boil 2-3 minutes. Add shrimp to water and boil 2-3 minutes or until shells begin to separate from shrimp. Drain, and serve by (are you ready for this?) pouring it in a heap on newspapers spread down the length of the table. Provide plates, forks, knives, butter, shrimp sauce, and napkins, lots of napkins.

We had gotten all the ingredients for the feast ready early in the afternoon so at dinnertime all we had to do was put the water in the pot, put the pot on to boil, add the meat and vegetables, wash up, and sit down to eat. Before putting the water in the pot I went to the basement to fetch a jar of green tomato pickles to accompany the meal and was met at the bottom of the basement stairs by a growing pool of water coming from the laundry room. Seems the water pipe had burst under the floor of the basement and the water from the pump had to be shut off immediately. We had no water for any purpose whatsoever. A dozen hungry, thirsty, tired people for dinner and no restroom, no sink, no water to drink. No problem! Off to our son Mark's house for water, behind the buildings in the back yard for resting-room, and canned and bottled beverages to quench their thirst. Luckily I'd made two apple pies in the afternoon so, in keeping with my motto which says, "Life is uncertain; eat dessert first," we all had pie and cheese. When the boil was done we poured those gorgeous red potatoes, that perfect pink shrimp, that honest brown sausage and that glowing yellow sweet corn down the middle of the table in an utterly beautiful heap and sat down— gratefully—to eat. When our guests saw that heap of food pile on

182

the table they gasped! In shock? Dismay? Delight? Amusement? Disgust? I don't know, but they all fell to and ate with gusto, after taking pictures of the pile.

Bertram brought the 90-minute documentary, which resulted from that month of work, back to Kansas City for a premiere in May of 1996. The documentary has since been shown at several European film festivals and has received rave reviews. It is being distributed in this country by California Newsreels at 149 Ninth St., San Francisco, CA 94103. For some reason, Bertram didn't include any footage of our boil in the film.

After this documentary aired in Germany, members of the press were compelled to write the following reviews:

"It won't help much to be prepared to face Jane Elliott. This elderly woman will tear down any shield. Even we, the spectators in BLUE EYED, can't get rid of this feeling of uneasiness, embarrassment, anxiety and utterly helpless hatred when she starts keeping people down, humiliating them, deriding them, incapacitating them. No doubt about this: for three quarters of the time in this documentation Jane Elliott is the meanest, the lowest, the most detestful, the most hypocritical human-being hell has ever spit back on earth. But she should be an example for all of us. *Stuttgarter Zeitung. 16.1.1997*

"BLUE EYED is not only a forceful appeal against discrimination, against the safe conscience of the nondiscriminated, but also the portait of a committed woman." *Junge Welt 5.12.1996*

"BLUE EYED is more than just Jane Elliott's story. It is a journey through an emotional maze. Few films can claim that they have the power to change somebody's life. Guaranteed, this one will." *The Desert Sun, Palm Springs 26.1.1997*

22 Not All That Glitters...

It was also in May of 1996 that I had my most unpleasant experience with a television talk show, when I had the misfortune of allowing myself to be roped into doing the "Nightline" show with Ted Koppel. Now, bear in mind that I was old enough to know better, and have no one to blame but myself. That said, I found the behaviors of the Koppel group reprehensible.

One of the Koppel's people called me in early April and said, "Ted wants someone to come on the show who will keep his Pat Buchanan followers from turning to the Leno Show after the first 10 minutes. Can you do that for him?"

"Sure," I laughed. "I can. But I won't. I don't do talk shows anymore, but I can give the names of several people who might." So I advised him to call C. T. Vivian, Ellis Cose, or Claude Steele, any one, or all of whom would be a great addition to any show dealing with the subject of the tension between people of color and white people in this society. He took their names and locations and then asked me if I planned to do the Blue-Eyed, Brown-Eyed exercise anytime in the near future and I said I didn't, but that I did have to present a three-hour lecture at several colleges and universities in the near future. Most of the presentations were to be for students, but the one at Northern Arizona University in the latter part of April was to be for staff and auxiliary personnel. He said he'd call the people I'd suggested. Could he call me later? Of course. I'd be interested in hearing who he'd booked. Several days later he called and said that they'd called those I'd suggested but that they'd really rather book me. I told him again that I wasn't interested. Then he asked if I'd allow them to video tape my lecture at the NAU and use some of that and some of the footage from Eye of the Storm, with, perhaps, interviews with some of the students from "Eye." That sounded reasonable to me, since I wouldn't be being interviewed by Koppel, so I gave him the name of my contact person, Sue Sager, at NAU and the deal was done. So I thought.

On April 24th a really delightful film crew came to NAU with the cooperation of Sue Sager and filmed my three-hour presentation. That, as far as I was concerned, was the end of my involvement with "Nightline." Not so. They took the tape of the presentation back to their offices and looked at it and called to ask if I'd please just agree to visit on remote with my former students as part of the show. They'd contacted Donna and Raymond and both had agreed to do the interview. It sounded like a winner to the "Nightline" people. Okay, if it was going to be a complete and coherent discussion of the anatomy of prejudice-and as they'd described it-I could work with them. In the meantime I'd gotten a copy of the Denkmal film and I told Koppel's representative about it. He wanted to see it immediately so we overnighted it to him and they arranged to purchase the use of several minutes of that film for use on the show.

On the morning of the airing of the show two remote crews pulled into our yard, one from Minneapolis (they'd been here before when Peter Jennings named me a "Person of the Week") and one from Chicago. They had been at the house for about half an hour when one of Koppel's people called me from Des Moines to tell me that he had just flown in from Washington DC and they'd changed the plans for the show. They had decided not to have my former students visiting with me and Koppel, but instead, to have Robert Woodson, the poster child of the conservative Republicans, debate me on camera. I told him to go back to D.C,, that this was exactly what I had told them originally that I would not do. The whole thing was a sham. He asked me to send the crews away and said he'd call DC. A short time later he called again and said he'd gotten everything straightened out and he was on his way to our house. Upon his arrival at our house, a couple of hours later, I asked him, "Is this show going to be as it was originally described to me?"

He said, "We need to talk." So we went into the kitchen and he told me that Woodson and I would not be debating but that Woodson would be making some comments during the show. I was more than disgusted. I knew, by then, that I was being used, but I also knew that this was a chance to get <u>Blue Eyed</u> on TV, so like a fool, I agreed to go ahead. And so we did.

Unfortunately, Koppel's first question for me was what I thought of the three shows they'd done so far that week. I thought they were dreadful. Koppel was less than pleased. After he finished a long and convoluted and – in my opinion – typical white male rationalization for unacceptable behaviors, we got into the interview. He questioned me for about twenty minutes, thanked me, and bade me goodnight. Then, his executive producer came on and asked me how I thought the interview had gone. I told him that I considered it a waste of my time and his money. I thought Koppel heard me, and when I watched the show that evening I was sure he had. It was one of the worst hatchet jobs I've ever seen. And it was so obvious an attempt to pander to the Pat Buchanan types that I actually laughed. At the very end of our interview in the afternoon I had slightly smiled and flexed my mouth to lick my lips which had become dry during our conversation. On camera it looked like I'd developed a twitch. Naturally, they left that on the show. Such a petty thing to do! I laughed again. How threatened did they feel that they had to resort to getting even in that way?

Bertram Ver Hoeg didn't laugh at the way they used his footage. He was simply furious. How could Koppel use Bertram's pictures and Koppel's voiceover? He'd never seen anything so unethical. Well, my dad used to say that all education is expensive, but the cheapest education you get is that which you pay for with money. I don't know what Bertram learned from this experience, but the lesson for me was: Never criticize a Koppel. But, you see, I've forgotten the lesson already! However, I've been reinforced in something I've felt for some time, which is that television is like a pan of milk: The cream rises to the top, but so does the scum.

23 The Best Laid Plans Go Oft Astray

During the last week in May of 1996 I spent three of the most interesting days I've ever known. On Tuesday of that week I flew to New York City to meet with Susan Golenbock, the entertainment lawyer with whom I've been working for three years; Susan Sarandon, the Hollywood star who is famous for her role, in among other movies, <u>Dead Man Walking</u>; and Bob Tabian, a literary agent who thinks he can find a market for this book. I hadn't met Susan Golenbock before, but after hearing her voice so often on the telephone I was sure I knew what she looked like: She'd be tall and rawboned with long, wavy, medium brown hair, and would walk with a no-nonsense stride swinging a briefcase from her long slim hand.

Mary McDonald, whom I admire greatly and who is part of Admire Presentations, which is the talent agency which represents me to colleges and universities, met me at the plane in the company of this short, plumpish, pretty, black-wavy-haired, sharp-eyed gremlin to whom I said, while sticking out my hand, "And you are?"

God's nightgown, such a greeting! It was Susan Golenbock, an utterly charming, knowledgeable human being with a terrific sense of humor and more common sense in her eyelashes than more people have in their entire anything! Susan and Mary took me out to dinner with Barbara Mayer and Trish Graziano, both of whom I had met several years ago as I worked with Admire

Presentations. I discovered once again during our dinner the total joy of being in the company of really bright, sparky, ambitious accomplished young women. What a group! No games, no power struggles, no jockeying for position, no ego trips, no one-upmanship. Just great conversation and real listening to one another. After dinner—delicious food in a place that looked like a warehouse almost redone—and specific instructions from Mary as to what I should not say the next day, general instructions from Susan as to what I should, Barbara and Susan dropped me off at the hotel. I went to bed fully aware that both Mary and Susan were convinced that I was a loose cannon and they were going to have to do some major damage control when I left town. I said the Serenity prayer half a dozen times and didn't go to sleep (no, I'm not an alcoholic, but that prayer has gotten me through a lot of tense times in these past few years.).

The next morning I ate a strange dieter's delight bland and boring breakfast (Why is so much of this book concerned with food?) and then took a taxi to Pliny Porter's office at Shoelace Productions, the company which is planning on producing the movie about the BE/BE exercise. The production company is located in an old narrow 12+ story building which appears to be very sparsely occupied. I rode up in an elevator with a blond, thin, personable-but-not-pushy young woman who said she worked for Shoelace, and who, therefore, knew how to gain admittance to their offices. This would not be an easy task for the casual visitor. We stepped off the elevator and then into another warehouse-like area separated into large, and for the most part airy, rooms decorated in sensible, attractive, calm and comfortable woods and books and posters and memorabilia and the reminders of labors of love. Nothing Hollywood! I was immediately impressed with Pliny Porter and the people he works with. We visited for a bit and then walked a couple of blocks to a terrific restaurant to meet Susan Sarandon. As the maitre d' led us to the tables in the back of the room we passed an antipasto (why isn't that prefix 'ante'?) buffet that should have a movie all its own.

He indicated that we could sit at any of the empty tables and when I told him that I wanted to sit with my back to the wall, he responded, "This is an Italian restaurant. Everyone who eats here wants to sit with their backs to the wall." I whipped my head around, wondering if I dared to laugh and he grinned at me and said, "Just joking. Just joking," as he seated us in a corner table—with my back to the wall.

A few minutes later he led Susan Sarandon to our table. I had thought she was tall and broad-shouldered. After all, hadn't she bested Tommy Lee Jones in <u>The Client</u>? Not tall. Not broad-shouldered. Average height, slim, energetic, not perky (I hate perky), businesslike, friendly, and preoccupied. Not disinterested; but busy-minded. Thinking of many issues and details while listening to me describe what I do and how and why I do it. Practical, pragmatic, precise and professional. No nonsense and no schmoozing! I'm impressed. This woman is like barbed wire with an electrical charge. Energetic. Dynamic. Wired! She said she wants to do this move about the BE/BE exercise and she wants to get started as soon as possible. I'm amazed and excited and concerned.

What if they try to make this story more exciting by adding some agony and sex and violence. What if they make me look like a cruel and heartless monster? What if, even more frightening, they portray me as this naïve, Pollyannaish well-meaning but misguided and ineffective waif? What if they make it too preachy? What if, on the other hand, they try so hard to avoid preaching that the message is lost? What if – and this is my greatest concern – they make a movie that treats discrimination of all kinds as the problem, thereby sidestepping yet again the issue of racism in this society, in an effort to avoid offending white viewers and reviewers? The exercise was and is primarily about racism, not only because that was the reason for Martin Luther King, Jr.'s death, which was the original impetus for using the exercise, but also because the way we treat people of color serves as a model for how we treat all those others--- women, the aged, those with disabilities, gay and lesbians, those who are other than Christians---who are physically or philosophically different from white Christian males. The movie must make the point that discrimination based on physical differences over which one has no control is very different from that based on religion or profession or socio-economic level. All those are factors which can be chosen and can be changed. They shouldn't have to be changed in order for one to be accepted in society, but they can be. Color, age, gender, sexual orientation and physical disabilities are seldom chosen and are difficult---in most cases, impossible---to change. As it happens, my concern was for naught. The film didn't get made, but I had a great time meeting Susan Sarandon and the women connected with Admire Entertainment.

24 Rehabilitating the Rehabilitators

One of the most interesting exercises I've ever conducted was with a group of Iowa Department of Corrections employees. It was to be part of their program aimed at making the overwhelmingly white prison employees sensitive to minority group issues and concerns. In a state where fewer than 3 percent of the population are members of minority groups, and minority groups make up over 20 percent of the prison population, the number of minority group members who work in the prisons is far smaller than the proportion who are incarcerated in them. The exercise was to be held in the conference center of an Iowa City motel. The forty – mostly white – employees were told that the conference was to be an all-day workshop on human relations.

At that time, we were using the term 'human relations,' but in the years since those few attempts at defusing the problem, we have had to keep changing the title in order to prevent the participants from complaining about 'yet another training session on racism.' While I was doing the exercise in various places and with various corporations, the title went from human relations, to pluralism, to cultural pluralism, to cultural diversity training, to one of the latest, and most unthreatening titles, white privilege.

The people involved in the training that morning were prison guards, supervisors, probation officers, parole officers, counselors, instructors, a cook, a maintenance worker, and a prison storekeeper. It was a group reminiscent of the group who went through the exercise at the White House Conference on Children and Youth, 18 years earlier. Unfortunately for this group, I had honed my skills and practiced my meanness and I was ready for whatever they could throw at me. Or so I thought.

The members of the group came in expecting to listen to a discussion of how they should go about dealing with those who were different from themselves, as they received printed materials which they would, or would not be responsible for responding to. They knew what to expect. After all, hadn't they been here before? It was a day away from the job, and they would be paid, whether or not they learned anything.

How confused they seemed when in the process of registering and receiving name cards, the group was divided according to eye color, of all things, and those with blue eyes were given ugly green collars, were told to wear them throughout the workshop, and were left standing in the hallway, as the non-blues were escorted into the dining area, where, in sight of the Blueys, they sat around and talked while they ate sweet rolls and drank coffee, juice, or tea. There were chairs in a stack in the hall, but the Blueys were told to use only those chairs which were not in the stack, and to make do with the few individual chairs that were available.

At nine o'clock, the Browns were politely asked to enter the conference room, while the Blues were left standing in the hall. No explanation was given; it was expected the Blueys would know enough to stay in their place and to be grateful that they were allowed to be at the conference at all, in view of how hard it is to teach a Bluey anything. There were signs on the restroom doors indicating that they were for "Browns Only." Blues who needed to relieve themselves were told to go either up one flight or down one flight of stairs, but only after they had signed out, so that the conference security people could keep track of them. This was not done to be mean to them; it was for their own good. After all, if something got lost, stolen, or broken in the hotel during this conference, we needed to be able to deny that any of the IDC people had been the guilty parties. There were no ashtrays for the Blueys, as we were trying to discourage them from indulging in that unsavory habit while at an IDC conference.

The conference room, also, had been set up to accommodate the two groups, one made up of ambitious, punctual, attentive, alert Browns, and one made up of self-indulgent, lackadaisical, rather disinterested Blues. The Browns were asked to sit in the front rows of chairs, due to their obvious desire to learn, and the Blues were going to be assigned to the back section of chairs so that their inability to pay attention would be less obvious to the superior group. That there were too few chairs for the Blues was not deliberate; you just never expect all those Blues who are scheduled to attend these meetings to show up, so why make arrangements for their presence?

I prepared the Browns by telling them that the purpose of the exercise was to give the Blues the opportunity to walk in the shoes of a person of color for a few hours. Therefore, the rules were designed to create a reality for these mostly white people, which they had probably never experienced before, but which many of the people of color in the prison – prisoners as well as employees – had been accustomed to for many years. Blue-eyed people were not to sit in the empty chairs in the Brown section. They were not allowed to sit next to the Browns at any time. Since, having been employed in the prison system in the state for several years, the Browns all knew how untrustworthy Blues are. They were to put their purses and other valuable possessions where the Blues would not be tempted to take them. I reminded them that Blues don't smell good, since they have little access to, or desire for, things like soap and deodorant. And, of course they were reminded that you never know what you might catch from a blue-eyed person.

I asked the Browns to relate some of the experiences they had had with Blues that would help all of us to justify our treatment of the Blues. The Browns, particularly the few blacks in the group, understood immediately what was being planned and executed and agreed, with some obvious delight, to help to educate the Blues to a new reality.

Those Browns who were supervising the Blues in the hall told me that by 9:30, the Blues began to be slightly annoyed. By 10:00 o'clock, they were making suggestions such as barging into the room and demanding that they be treated fairly. One thought they should just all go home, since they weren't going to be part of the discussion which was obviously taking place in the conference. That got no support; after all, this was their job assignment for the day, and to leave would be to sacrifice the day's pay. One woman suggested that they all sing loudly, a song of defiance. The suggestion to sing "We Shall Overcome," was rejected immediately, luckily for them. It would have been good for me to have them usurp the song emblematic of the Civil Rights Movement, but really bad for them.

Upon entering the conference room, the Blueys were told to leave their belongings on the floor at the back of the room. As Pat Okura, said in Washington, DC, at the White House Conference on Children and Youth, "You never know what they might be carrying in those bags and purses, you know."

The Browns watched with ill-concealed contempt as the Blues did exactly as they were told. Their attention, however, as they looked for places to sit in their section, in which there were too few chairs for them to sit, was directed to the large, colorful signs on the walls of the room. They were simply the signs which have been used as discriminatory slogans in this country for many years, and of course, should have been seen as non-offensive by adult, reasonable, sensible people. They said things like, "If I have only one life to live, let me live it as a Brown," and "I'm not prejudiced; some of my best friends are Blue-eyed." Another said, "I'm free, Brown-eyed, and over twenty-one." There was one of the ever-popular, "Let in one Blue-eye and there goes the neighborhood."

The Blueys spent several minutes milling about at the back of the room, and, when it was obvious that there weren't enough chairs for them in that area, they began to drift into the Brown section. Naturally, they were told to stay in their place, and, when one of the Blue-eyed males picked up a chair and tried to take it back to his section, he was roundly criticized and told to go back to his place and either stand or sit on the floor at the back of the room.

As they finally got organized and the room had quieted down, I announced, "In the future, it would be to your advantage if you'd get to meetings on time." Not one Bluey complained or reminded me that they were late, not because they ran on Blue-eyed time, but because we had systematically kept them out of the room. When I noticed that a well-dressed young woman was chewing gum, I added, "It would also be to your advantage if you'd get rid of that gum. Third-graders know that good listeners have quiet hands, feet, and mouths. I expect you to know at least as much as a third-grader."

"I'll leave," the young woman threatened, with a toss of her head.

"If you stay, you'll put your gum away," I said.

"I'll leave," the woman repeated, this time with that air of defiance that we see so often in Blueys, when they're doing the wrong thing at the wrong time.

"Do you want to get paid for today?" I asked.

The wanna-be rebel nodded.

"Then put your gum away," I said, with exaggerated patience.

"I don't have a purse, so I don't have a place to put my gum." The Bluey complained, once again, of course, blaming it on me that she had been told to put her purse at the back of the room, instead of taking the responsibility for coming into a learning environment chewing gum. Everyone knows that that behavior is unacceptable in the workplace, and that chewing gum or eating candy in a learning situation is a signal that the miscreant is in his/her child ego state, and not prepared to learn.

"I'm sure you're inventive enough to find a place for that gum," I said, trying to give her the benefit of the doubt.

At that, not surprisingly, the foolish Bluey took the gum from her mouth and stuck it on the bottom of her chair.

That was the worst possible thing she could have done at that moment, for it gave me the opportunity to say to the Browns, who had been watching this exchange with much curiosity and, I think, a little trepidation, "You have this problem with blue-eyed people. You give them something nice and they just wreck it. You'll also notice that blue-eyed people spend a lot of time playing 'Look at me. See how funny I am. I can be funny. I can make a joke of this. You can't bother me. I find this amusing.

Another thing that you have to do with these blue-eyed people is teach them the listening skills, since it's obvious by their behaviors, that they don't know them." I then began to dictate the listening skills which are a staple in my classroom, wherever I teach, and which I expected the entire group to write down. As I dictated the first listening skill, "Good listeners have quiet hands, feet, and mouths," I noticed a blue-eyed man in the back, leaning lazily against the wall, eyes on the ceiling, and hands in his pocket.

"I'd like for all of you to look at the man in the black jacket in the back of the room," I said. Everyone turned to look, the Browns expectantly, the Blues in dread. "This boy's game is called, 'playing it cool,' 'Nobody can bother me, man. I can handle this. You can't make me mad, and you can't make me learn, either. I'm just gonna ignore the whole thing."

The man in black looked at me for just an instant and then looked quickly away. Finally, rather than look me in the eye, he looked at the floor and then ran his hand down his face, no longer disinterested, but annoyed.

I continued to dictate the listening skills, which the brown eyed people studiously wrote down, but it quickly became apparent that the blue-eyes weren't writing. Of course they weren't; I'd set them up by telling them to leave their coats and purses on the floor at the back of the room. Did any of them have the temerity to remind me of that? Of course not. So, with their tacit approval for what I was doing to them, I suggested that those who'd had the good sense to keep their learning materials with them might be willing to share some pencils with the less innovative members of their group.

Naturally, the man in black made no effort to borrow a pencil, and I said to him, "Sir, I realize that you feel you don't need to write this down, but whether or not you want to do the work that the others are doing, perhaps you will try to remember this information."

"I'll borrow a pen," he said.

"Good listeners have quiet hands, feet, and mouths," I repeated. "Do you know what that means?" I knew I was pushing him, and I didn't know how far I dared to go, but I was glad there were security people in the room, as I could see that he was getting more than a little impatient with this needling.

"I'm not sure," he replied, turning away from the wall.

"I believe that," I said. "Do you want me to explain it to you?"

Unbelievably, at that point, he said, "That's okay. I'll get a pencil and write this down directly."

"Look, you blue-eyed people," I said to those blucys seated near him, "Some of you have extra pencils. Will at least one of you lend him one for a few minutes? Or don't you trust him? Which I can understand." Then, I turned to the brown-eyed people and asked, "In the last ten minutes, what have you learned about blue-eyed people, just from watching their behaviors?"

"Blue-eyed people are very stubborn," a tall black man in the front row said. "You have to realize that they're very self-centered and wish to control as much of their surroundings as they can—people wise, I mean. Very inconsiderate people. I don't know why we have to have them here, in the first place."

"We only have them here because we're required to." I replied.

"We have to, eh?"

"This is one of the things you have to put up with when you work in a government agency," I sighed.

As the exercise progressed and I continued to treat the blue-eyed people as inferiors, using all the techniques I had learned as a white person with power, the brown-eyed participants joined in. A brown-eyed white woman described her two nephews, one of whom was blue-eyed, the other brown-eyed.

"He never cleans his room and he's real lazy, that blue-eyed one. He doesn't seem to have a lot of energy. But the brown-eyed one, is real outgoing. He plays in sports and he's real good at whatever he does. He just seems like a better kid. So, if I have kids, I hope they have brown eyes."

"Are you married?" I asked, just barely hiding the disgust that I was feeling for her being able to voice this racist crap so coolly. It was obvious that she was repeating something like what she'd been hearing for a long time.

"No."

"Then it's a good thing you don't have kids, isn't it?

"Right," the woman replied.

"But you'll know what to do when you choose a mate."

"Yeah," the woman replied, totally oblivious to the sarcasm in my voice.

When I had finished dictating the listening skills, I asked the man in the back who had been referred to as Roger by one of the participants to read the first listening skill aloud.

"I haven't got it on my paper yet," he said, turning halfway away from the wall.

"Oh, why is that?" I asked.

"I haven't borrowed the pencil to write it down, as yet."

"And you regard these rules and this assignment as unnecessary?"

"Well, at this particular point, yes I do," he said with obvious indignation and annoyance.

"Why is that?" I asked again, delighted, now, at his increasingly disgusted attitude.

Most of the people in the room, both blue- and brown-eyed had turned to look at him again and he saw their attention and their facial expressions. Were they amused? Some seemed to be teetering on indecision. What to do? He was their friend, in some cases, and their co-worker. Were they sympathetic? Did they not dare to speak up? Why were they allowing me to treat him this way, and why didn't they offer him some encouragement, if not support? I could see him looking at his 'friends' as if to say, "Why are you just sitting there? Why don't you argue with this woman? Finally, he just shook his head, at a loss for any answer, much less an appropriate answer in this utterly confusing situation. Finally, he said, "Well, I have it in my head for the most part."

"Well," I pressed him, "There's a lot of space up there for it, isn't there? But, since you haven't made the attempt to write it down, perhaps you could tell me what it is."

"It has something to do with having your hands and feet still, as I recall, "It has something to do with that," When this elicited laughter from the blue-eyed group, I turned quickly to the group, knowing that laughter, at this point, was a way of releasing the tension that was building up in the room, which was exactly what I couldn't let occur.

"I find that highly interesting. Stupid, but interesting." Then, turning my attention to the brown-eyed group, to ward off the chance for any of the blue-eyed participants to defend him, asked, "If you are in a situation where someone is constantly refusing to do what the people in authority require them to do, what do you assume about that person"?"

One brown-eyed white man, in a business suit spoke up, "I think it's a game with them," he said. "He'll do anything to get attention."

"Has he gained anything at this point?" I asked.

"He's gained disrespect from the brown-eyed people," he replied.

"Has he proven anything to the brown-eyed people, by his behavior? I asked.

"Yes," the man replied. "He's proven that this is typical behavior from a blue-eyed person."

Turning once more to Roger, I said, "Now, the second one," fully knowing that he didn't have the second listening skill, either.

"I don't have the second one," Roger said, less truculently.

"You don't have the second one, either?"

"No."

"You were keeping it in your head," I reminded him, wondering how long he would tolerate this badgering. "What happened to that plan?"

"Just the first one I had in my head," Roger said, by now practically incoherent at the position in which he found himself. "Not the second one."

"Oh, the other three aren't important?" I persisted.

"Well, they're probably important, Roger admitted.

"But not important enough for you to bother either to write them down, or to remember them, right?"

"Well," Roger ground out, "they're important. I should've written them down, most probably."

"Most probably?" I mimicked. Then, turning to the brown-eyed people, I asked, "What do you know about blue-eyed people that you didn't know before we started this lesson?"

"Well," turning in his chair slightly, to roll his head back towards Roger, "I'm finding out that I'm going to have to explain things a bit more explicitly to a blue-eyed person than I am to a brown-eyed person." My thought, at that moment was to wonder at the callousness of his behavior toward his friend and peer. Where was this coming from and how would he justify it later on?

"How many times did I have to repeat the listening skills for Roger?" I asked.

Now the man turned to look at Roger and said, "Well, brother Roger is having a rough time, today, isn't he? It was about six or seven times, wasn't it?

Did I correct the brown-eyed man, for his exaggeration? No, he was doing what he knew was the right thing to do in this situation, and I figured he was acting and speaking from his own experiences in the world outside this room. And he was obviously taking some delight in doing so.

Later, I handed out the Dove Counterbalance Test, a written test that is deliberately biased in favor of American blacks, and designed to let white people know how it feels to have your intelligence judged by how well you can respond to a set of questions about which you know very little, sometimes practically nothing. Unbeknownst to the blue-eyed group, I had given the browns the answers to the even numbered questions on the test, before the blues came into the room. This was not something I had simply made up; it was what I had seen happen, ever since I got involved with this work. It's a simple technique: Give a group of people a test composed of a vocabulary and information that is utterly foreign to them and, when they don't know the answers, blame their ignorance on their age, their gender, or the color of their skin. We do it all the time, with great success, and the approval of other people who want a group to live down to our expectations of them.

When all had completed the test, I took the blue-eyed participants' papers from them and gave them to the brown-eyed people to correct, remarking as I did so, that it was unfortunate that the browns had to do this extra work, but that's how it is when you work with inferior people. After all, you can't let them check their own, or their blue-eyed peers' tests because they'd cheat on the checking, in order to prove us wrong about them. Then, I read each participant's name off the class roll, as the browns read their scores off the tests. Of course, the browns got very good scores, while the blues got exactly the scores that we all expected them to get. It was at this point that the gum-chewing Bluey decided to assert herself, again.

A brown-eyed man, who had checked a test reported a score of only eleven correct responses on test and reported the name on the test as the initials, "K. R."

"K. R.?" I asked. "Just initials? No first or last name?"

"No names," the man said reluctantly. At that the blue-eyed gum chew stood up to claim the paper. When another brown-eyed man had trouble reading the name of another blue-eyed woman, that woman identified herself and took her paper from him. The brown-eyed woman reported the score of a paper signed only "E. Riley." The three women whose tests had been incorrectly labeled were sitting together in a tight little group, and I said to the three of them,

"You know, what you do to the image of blues, with your behavior, is unfortunate, but what you three women do to the image of women with your ineptitude really makes me angry. The fact that you do this kind of sloppy work reflects badly on all women and I resent that doubly."

At this point, K.R. leaned forward, and with an exaggerated air of civility and supplication, said, "Ma'am, I'd really appreciate it if you'd call us by name. When you say 'you three people' we don't know who you are speaking to. It could be anyone here."

"My dear," I answered with equally exaggerated civility, "if you wanted me to call you by your name, you'd have put your name on your paper."

"It's on my coat," K. R. said holding up the nametag on the lapel of her suit jacket.

"It was to be on your paper," I reminded her, impatiently.

"You didn't see my paper, ma'am."

"I didn't see your name, either, because it wasn't on your

paper." I replied, becoming a trifle testy. This broad was getting on my nerves and, although she was certainly nailing down the idea that blues don't know how to behave in an instructional setting, she was also slowing down the process.

"That's alright."

"All right," I said, "Now, how could one call you by your name if you don't care enough about your name to put it on your paper?"

"You can't even read?" K. R. asked, sarcastically, pointing again to her name tag.

"Don't expect me to worry about it if you don't put it on your paper. Don't sit there and say, 'My name is important to me,' after you have just deliberately *not* put it on your paper." I was then and I'm even more amazed now, at how childishly she was behaving, how determined she was to blame her mistake on someone else, and how similar her actions were to people in my school who were constantly making excuses for what they did, and didn't want to, do. Were the rest of the employees recognizing what was going on here? Was this the way she behaved on a daily basis in the workplace?

"I don't remember saying my name was important to me," K.R. said, icily. "I remember saying I'd like to know who you're speaking to when you say, 'you three'."

"Then what should you do?" I asked.

"Ask that you use my name, which I did." In other words, K.R. had to prove to all and sundry that she was in no way responsible for doing anything negative or unacceptable; she was being unfairly accused of having made a mistake.

"And where should your name have been?" I asked, knowing full well that she was not going to admit to having been wrong.

"Right here where it is," K.R. said, holding up her name tag once more. "And on my birth certificate."

"Is it on your paper?" I asked.

"No ma'am." Now she was using a term that is often used to feign respect when it is actually supposed to put the one being addressed into the position of an unwelcome supervisor, who has to be obeyed, but not respected. Did K.R. know how typical of a fractious child her behavior was? Did she realize that she had been reduced to her child ego state and that she was trying to achieve the parent ego state against impossible odds? How far was I willing to push? I decided to go one step further.

"Where'd you get a birth certificate?" I asked.

K.R. hesitated only an instant, "Out of a slot machine," she snapped. If she had stopped right there, she'd have avoided an opportunity to have me make her look even more foolish. She didn't stop. "Same as you did, lady."

"I think you're probably right about your own," I said.

"At least I know who my parents are, ma'am," K.R. said angrily.

Addressing an Asian man in the brown-eyed group, I asked, "Is she being rude?" I deliberately did not use her name; she hadn't earned the right to be addressed or described as she would have preferred.

"Yes," he answered.

"Is she being inconsiderate?"

"Yes."

"Is she being insulting?"

"Yes."

"Are those all the things that we've accused blue-eyed people of being?"

"Yes."

"Is she proving that we're right?"

"Yes."

Encouraged, perhaps emboldened, by K.R.'s defiance, a blue-eyed man spoke up, not to defend her, but to ask, "Do you feel that there are important blue-eyed people?" In other words, I felt that he was asking me to agree that not all blues are as insignificant and unreasonable as she was being.

"There are exceptions to every rule," I replied.

"And what are those exceptions?" he asked.

"There are a few important blue-eyed people," I answered.

"Do you think you are one of them?" a blue-eyed woman asked.

"No," I answered immediately.

"Then why are you up there?" asked the man who had first raised the question.

"I'm blue-eyed," I answered unapologetically. "The difference between you and me is, I have a brown-eyed husband

and brown-eyed offspring, and I've learned how to behave in a brown-eyed society. And when you can act brown enough, then you, too, can be where I am."

That was obviously too much for K.R. "I wouldn't want to be where you are," she said, in a manner that belied what she was saying. Did she not recognize that she was doing exactly what defiant dyslexic boys, some people of color, and a whole lot of women do every day, in reaction to being treated unfairly on the basis of physical characteristics over which they have no control? Didn't she recognize that she was being controlled by me, by the browns, and the set-up in the room? Did she really think that the way she was handling this experience is the way black males handle what happens to them? Did she not realize that being this belligerent, defiant, and rude would have gotten a black male evicted from the situation in a few minutes? Had she any idea of how easy it is for people of color to get into places where they are supervised by people like herself?

"Are you certain that you wouldn't want to be where I am?" I asked, giving her a chance to recant.

"Absolutely positive."

"You like where you are?"

"I love where I am." No one believed her, but she had talked herself into a hole and had no way out of it.

"You like it so much that you don't even put your name on your paper," I commented.

"I don't need to, lady," K.R. snapped.

This was the second time she had called me 'lady' and this time I couldn't let it pass. For many years, the word has been used to keep women in their place. There is a standard of behavior for ladies, which women don't have to adhere to. I decided it was time to take notice of her use of the word, and the ignorance she was exhibiting by using it, instead of dealing with her feeble attempts to justify her refusal to put her name on her paper. I turned to the brown-eyed group and asked, "Her use of the term 'lady' where I'm concerned – what do you think she's trying to do? Is it ignorance, or is it just deliberately insulting?"

"I would say it was deliberately insulting," a brown-eyed woman said.

Grateful for the support, I said, "If it's ignorance, she needs to be taught that, to many of us, the word 'lady' is a pejorative. It's a pejorative. It's a putdown, particularly when it's said in the tone of voice she's using. Most of us have had that treatment and didn't appreciate it. I certainly don't appreciate it."

"I will call you by the correct name, after this," K.R. promised. "I won't be kind." Oh Lord, this woman can't let it go, and she's fighting a battle she can't win, since I'm going to change the rules, if she begins to make progress. I hope she's learning something about resistance and powerlessness, here.

"That was kindness on your part?" I asked in disbelief.

"Yes," K.R. replied. "I think to call someone a lady is a kindness." In spite of all her years of being taught the Golden Rule? Was this the way she practiced that homily? I didn't dare to get into religion, at this point, but was she really treating me the way she wanted to be treated? If so, then the way I was treating her was just right. So why wasn't she happy? What was she so angry about? I was treating her unfairly and getting away with it, and she was reacting in a way that proved all the things I had said about blue-eyed people were true.

"Then your problem is ignorance."

"You can call me 'lady' anytime you like," K.R. sneered.

"I wouldn't do that to you."

"No, I know you wouldn't." Was she beginning to realize that the term 'lady' could not be applied to her at the present time, and in view of her behavior?

"I really wouldn't," I lied. "And that's part of the problem – a total lack of awareness of what sexism amounts to, and how much you contribute to the sexism that keeps you where you are today, and outside this room."

"I like where I am, lady," K.R. fired back. And then, realizing what she had said, she grinned like a recalcitrant schoolboy and said, "I did it again, didn't I?"

Now, the blue-eyed man who had tried to take a chair from the brown-eyed section at the beginning of the session spoke up for the first time, "I'm getting kind of fed up with this whole bunch of garbage," he said.

"Why?" I asked, but I was thinking, why did it take so long?

"Brown-eyed people are no different than we are," he said. "I hate to tell them that. They have these false delusions and such."

I could have kissed that blue-eyed boy, particularly in view of the fact that he was describing white behaviors perfectly. I'm not sure he meant to be doing that, but that was the way it looked to me.

"Are they being disruptive?" I asked.

"No," he conceded. "You've trained them very well. I think that's what they did with the storm troopers in Germany also." And then, addressing the brown-eyed people in the front of the room, "You guys did a real good job sitting up there."

"You think that what's happening here today feels the way it would have felt to be in Nazi Germany?" I asked.

"Yes," he replied.

"If we're in Nazi Germany, who are you?" I asked, gesturing at the blue-eyed group.

"The Jews," he said.

Was I grateful for his description of the situation? Oh, yes. Had I seen this reaction to the exercise before? Oh, yes. Did I hope that the rest of the group, both browns and blues, were relating what he was saying to the ugliness, not only of what happened during the Holocaust, but also to what is happening to the many black males who end up in the hands of the Iowa Department of Corrections? Oh, yes!

I had decided, after doing the exercise with groups of adults before, that reversing the exercise with them is too time-consuming and counter-productive. If you reverse the exercise with adults, it gives them the idea that this is just a game and that all they have to do is hang in there and they'll get their chance eventually. That's not the way the exercise works, because that's not the way society works. Since whites have been in the advantageous position, for the past 400 years, are we going to let people of color run the show, for the next 400 years? Obviously not, so, in order to maintain the reality of the exercise, I left the blues in the inferior position, while we went to lunch. After we came back from lunch, I announced to the participants that the first part of the workshop was over. "Now, let's talk about what happened this morning," I suggested. The tension that had pervaded the room disappeared, and within minutes, one after another of the blue-eyed people was struggling to express how the morning had felt – and why. Their relief at being released from their previous status was palpable. It was exactly the way my third-graders behaved when the exercise was over, and they could all get back together, again.

"Did you learn anything, this morning?" I asked Roger.

Roger, who had shed his black jacket, was now in the front of the room. "I think I learned from the experience a feeling like I was in a glass cage, and I was powerless. There was a sense of hopelessness. I was angry. I wanted to speak up, and yet I knew if I spoke up, I'd be attacked. I had a sense of hopelessness, depression." This statement from a man, part of whose job was to supervise people who spent their every day and night in a cage.

Turning to the brown-eyed group, I asked, "How did you brown-eyed people feel while this was going on?"

"I had a sense of relief that I wasn't a blue-eyed person," a man said immediately.

I nodded. I'd heard this from third graders every time I did the exercise. "A sense of relief that you had the right color eyes."

"Right."

"Absolutely," I said.

The blue-eyed man who asked if there were any important blue-eyed people said, "I really understood – at least I felt that I understood what it was like to be in the minority."

"Had you experienced that before?" I asked him.

"I realized this morning that there were very few times in my life that I've ever been discriminated against. Very few."

"And you were that uncomfortable in an hour and a half?"

"I was amazed at how uncomfortable I was in the first fifteen minutes," Roger spoke up.

"Can you empathize at all with blacks, minority group members in the country?"

"I'm hoping better than before," he replied.

David Stokesbury, the blue-eyed man who had drawn the analogy with Nazi Germany, said, "If we tried to argue with you, you would use the mere argument as proof that we were less than the brown-eyed folks. You know, you couldn't win."

"Yes, but don't we do that every day?" I asked.

"I think some do, yeah," he admitted. "But I hope that I would never get so unreasonable. You know, the statements you were making were groundless, and yet we couldn't argue with them, because if we argued, then we were argumentative and – you know – not listening and getting out of our place and all that stuff. And that was frustrating to me. And also frustrating to me was the other blue-eyed people who were sitting on their hands. My group here was, I don't think, boisterous enough in opposition to the whole thing."

I nodded, not only in agreement, but in total delight. I knew that I couldn't possibly have written a script for this video that would have been as good, and as valid, as what these participants were saying. No college professor's lecture could possibly have been as meaningful and honest as what these young people were saying. "Why didn't you people support one another," I asked.

"The blue-eyed people on this side of the room just sat there. And let's face it, you covered your asses. Right? Why did you just sit there?"

A blue-eyed man who had done just that spoke, "I think that's symptomatic of the problem as a whole. We see that, you know, in society in general. We see a few people who are making a lot of noise and the rest of the people sitting back waiting to see what they're going to do."

"As long as I was picking on him, I was leaving you alone. Right?" I asked.

"Right."

"I'd say a lot of people do that," a blue-eyed woman said. "They let a few people do their fighting for them, and they stand back, and if this person's going to win, then they'll get on his side. But if that person's not going to win, they'll stand back over here, you know. That's just how it works."

Not wanting to debate that fact with her, I turned back to the man, and said, "If you were in a real situation where you had to do something about racist behaviors, would you stand up and be counted?"

"*What* I would do, I don't know, he said. "It would depend on the circumstances."

"But you would so something?" I pressed him.

"I would *have* to do something. I couldn't go home and face my kids tonight, if I didn't."

K.R. had not spoken yet, and I wanted to see whether she had, indeed, learned anything from the position in which my 'society' had places her. "Why were you angry?" I asked her.

"First of all," she said, "because it was unreasonable. Secondly, because I felt discriminated against. Thirdly, I think that all of us – everyone in this room – has dealt with discrimination on both sides. (At this point, I was getting more that a little disgusted. Had she learned nothing, when she felt that she was being treated in an unreasonable and discriminatory way? Did she really think that her two hours in the hot seat was comparable to what people of color go through in this country, from birth to death? It got worse.) You don't have to be black or Jewish or Mexican or anything to have felt discrimination on your life. And as you become an adult, you learn to deal with those feelings within yourself, and you learn to handle those. And when you feel yourself in a situation that you can't get out of, which we couldn't – we were a captive audience, and it was not a normal situation, because normally you aren't badgered…" She ground to a halt, perhaps realizing that she was describing precisely the normal situation of many blacks.

"What if you had to spend the rest of your life this way?" I asked her.

K.R. shook her head. "I don't know how to answer that," she grudgingly admitted.

But a pale-skinned, black-haired woman in the row directly in front of her did. Speaking directly to K.R., she said, "You don't wake up every morning knowing that you're different. You wake up as a white woman, who is going to her job at eight o'clock or whatever. Where a black person is going to wake up knowing, from the minute that they get out of bed and look in the mirror, they're black, and they have to deal with the problem they've had to deal with ever since they were young – and realize that 'I'm different, and I have to deal with life differently.'" Then she went on to say, "I am black and I never told anyone that I was until two years ago."

"What happened when you told people the truth?" I asked.

"I lost all my friends," she replied. At that point, K.R. leaned forward and said to her, "I didn't know you were black."

"And what would you have done, if I had told you?" the young woman asked. K.R. gave a dismissive wave of her hand and sat back in her chair. The young woman went on, "And I don't think you can really say that you have felt – maybe you have felt some sort of discrimination – but you haven't felt what it is like for a black woman: to go through the daily experience of arguing and saying, 'Listen to me. My point of view is good, you know. What I have to offer here is good.' And no one wants to listen, because white is right. That's the way things really are." I was amazed at her courage for having spoken up this way. I was shocked at K.R.'s response to what she said. But, when I saw the finished film, I was infuriated, because her statement about being black had ended up on the cutting-room floor. I called Bill Peters, the producer of the show, and asked why he had left that moment out of the film. He said it was a time problem. I was beside myself with anger and disappointment. This wasn't the first time, nor would it be the last, that I was naïve and foolish, but in that moment, I was as angry and felt as betrayed as I ever have.

When the discussion began to lag, I spoke briefly about how the exercise works with young children and how similar the adults' responses were to what I elicit from children. I then ran the film, The Eye of the Storm for them. They had more questions about the exercise and more answers about their reactions to it. When I finally declared that the workshop was over, many of the Corrections Department employees lingered to talk some more. This is what happens every time I give a lecture or do the exercise. Participants seem to need to experience a catharsis, and those who have gone through the exercise with them have become people they trust to listen to the descriptions of what they've felt. A number of the participants on that day made it a point to thank me for the experience.

Several years after that workshop, I gave a speech to a group in Des Moines and, when I asked if there were any questions, a young woman at the back of the room stood up to tell me that she had driven for several hours to get to Des Moines in order to hear my words. As I recall, she said that 'Brother Roger' was her father and he had come home from that day a different person. When I asked her whether the changes were positive, or negative, she said they were positive and she thanked me for what I had done for her family. Just a few years ago, I did a telephone chat with a class in southern Iowa and 'Brother Roger' was there to share with the kids and me some of the ways his life has changed, as a result of the exercise.

The workshop and discussion following it once more validate my assertion that the mechanics for perpetuating a racist society are fairly simple: Pick out a group of people on the basis of a physical characteristic over which they have no control. Describe them as displaying all the negative traits we despise. Force them to live down to our expectations of them. When they do live down to our expectations, by getting angry and defensive and acting out, use their behaviors to prove that everything we said about them was true. We can prove to them and all those who witness the exchange that those stereotypes we are attempting to establish are, indeed, accurate.

I have been doing this exercise for just short of 50 years, with children of all ages, and the behaviors and results are invariably the same, no matter how young or how old the participants happen to be.

The thing that made me the most disgusted with this group was K. R.'s assertion that everyone has experienced some kind of discrimination and that as you became an adult you learn how to handle it. It seemed to me that she was saying that if other groups had overcome handicaps, why couldn't the minority groups in this country do the same? She also seemed to be saying that there is something in minority group members that makes it impossible for them to "grow up' and 'handle' their reactions to discrimination in an adult fashion—as she did in a short workshop.

Perhaps one day she will come to the conclusion that the way minority group members react to discrimination is not the result of some weakness in their genes, but is simply the way human beings react when they are treated unfairly because of something over which they have no control. What they actually have no control over is the ignorance of the majority group members who think that differences are bad, but that people, who are similar to themselves, must be good. Perhaps she will also come to realize that she was extremely upset over being mistreated for a couple of hours, and knew that the treatment was going to end when the workshop ended. People of color have been waiting for their workshop to end for 400 years, in this country.

I hope that anyone who reads this book will contact PBS and try to purchase a copy of that film. Or perhaps you'll contact the folks at PBS and ask them to show it in prime time, as they did for many years. It is a terrific learning and teaching tool.

Hopefully, one day we will manage to convince the world that 'race', meaning four or five different races of people, is a social construct and that we are all, in fact, members of the same race, which is, of course, the Human race. That race, while composed of many color groups, and many cultural groups, is still the race to which we all belong.

25 Something to Chew On

So what does all this mean? It means that using the eye-color exercise has provided me with some enlightening experiences which have caused me to draw some, what I consider logical conclusions. You can't deny my experiences, though some of you will try, but you can argue with my conclusions. So here is something for you to dispute:

1. We are not equal. I am not equal to any of the people I've met in these past 62 years; every one of them can do something I can't do or knows something I don't know. However, while we aren't equal, we are, in the USA, guaranteed equitable treatment under the law. I'm not demanding equality; I'm demanding equitable treatment for all of us and I want it now. Now some you will say that in the eyes of God, we are all equal. Fine, but while I talk to God constantly, I deal constantly with fallible human being like myself, and we are the ones responsible for guaranteeing equitable treatment to all.

2. The way white females and people of color react, is not because they are inferior to white males; it's the way human beings react when they are treated unfairly on the basis of a physical characteristic over which they have no control. I can turn adult white males into people who act the way minorities are accused of acting in fifteen minutes flat just by the way I arrange their environment. As the final piece of the BE/BE exercise in corporations, now, I ask the Browns, who represent the power

structure in this society, to write 3 adjectives that describe the say the Blues, who represent white women and people of color and others who are obviously different in this society, looked and acted during the exercise. I ask the Blues to write 3 adjectives describing how the Browns looked to them during the exercise. I get the same list of words no matter what the geographic location of the exercise is. These are the words Browns use to describe the Blues: distressed, insecure, docile, stupid, angry, confused, defensive, withdrawn, intimidated, unsure, inferior, rebellious, flailing, humiliated, frustrated and embarrassed. Notice how many of these are words that we usually use to describe, indeed, to define, women. And bear in mind that most of the participants in these exercises are adult white males. The words which the Blues write to describe the Browns are: arrogant, cold, hostile, condescending, aggressive, rude, uncaring, smug, ignorant and belligerent. Are these the words that people of color apply to us whites when we aren't in their presence? And if so, why?

3. Racism isn't a problem only of the uneducated, the poor or the lower class. They aren't the ones who run for elective office or who write and publish the textbooks or who produce the television shows or who teach in our schools. And all those entities contribute to the growing level of racism in this country.

4. Prejudice doesn't cause discrimination; discrimination causes prejudice. Pick out a group of people on the basis of a physical characteristic over which they have no control; assign negative traits to them on the basis of that physical characteristic; treat them as though all the negative things you're saying about them are absolutely true; when they react negatively to your treatment, blame their behaviors on their genes instead of on how they're being treated. You can convince not only them but everyone who witnesses their behaviors that you were right about them all along.

5. You weren't born a racist. Racism is a learned response; it is not genetic. Luckily, anything that is learned can be unlearned and it's way past time to unlearn our racism.

6. Love is not the answer to the problems of the "isms" in our society: the answer is justice. If we claim to love one another but do not treat one another justly, we will not have a loving society or a just one. However, if we treat one another justly, we may very well find ourselves coming to love one another because we have no reason not to! A Black man at the premiere of the film, Blue Eyed, in Kansas city stood during the discussion following the film and said to the group, "All I want is for whites to love and respect me." Look at the conundrum we have created in this society: on the one hand we teach that we must love one another and show respect for one another while at the same time we teach that only white people are truly loveable and deserving of respect. And we send that negative message throughout the media and the educational institutions, in our courts and our city councils, in our real estate associations and our lending institutions, in our libraries and our bookstores, in our country clubs and our fraternal organizations, in our military and our maternity wards, in our cathedrals and our country churches. What we do speaks so loudly that it's hard for people of color to hear what we say. And it's even harder for them to believe what we say. But they keep trying and I don't know why.

7. We don't have a 'black problem'. You can't blame 100 percent of the problem on 12 percent of the population unless you're prepared to admit that people of color have more power than white folks do. Skin color isn't the problem; white folks' ignorant reaction to skin color is the problem.

8. We don't need a colorblind society – unless there's something wrong with skin color. What we now have is a society that is blinded by color. White people have been and are continuing to be, conditioned to the myth of white superiority by the most

powerful institutions in our country: the government, the churches, the education system, and the entertainment industry. Those are the agencies that shape our environments, and as long as they are directed by people who see differences as negatives that's how long we will have racism in this country.

9. One person can make a difference. Watch any of the documentaries about this exercise, which you can find on my website: ***www.janeelliott.com***

10. You don't have to have people of color in your immediate surroundings to have racism. All you need for racism to exist is angry, vulnerable, insecure white people who have been conditioned by the governmental institutions to believe that their power is being threatened by those who are different from themselves.

11. Racism is a mental health problem. The President's Joint Council on Mental Health in Children identified racism as the number one mental health issue among children in the US in 1959. You see, if you base your worth as a human being – or judge other people's worth – on the basis of the amount of a chemical in your – or their – skin, you aren't dealing well with reality and you need to get some therapy. Soon.

12. White superiority is a myth that has been foisted on us by about five hundred years of conditioning calling itself education or, worse, history, or even worse, science. Now I realize that some of those who read this material will decide to write me a letter to tell me how wrong I am about this. Good idea. You do that. But if you're going to be a racist, you will want to give up all the things that people of color have made available for you.

So you'd best write this letter before dark, because many of the components for generating and transmitting electricity were invented by Black males. So you'll want to turn off your electric lights.

Now you're probably deciding that you'll light a candle. No, you won't. People of color had fire before white folks got cold.

So you'll wait until morning to write your letter, but don't use an alarm clock to help you to get up on time; people of color had time-measuring devices before white folks realized that time was passing.

Now, when you reach for that piece of paper on which to write your letters…stop! We got paper from the Chinese and the Egyptians, most of whom are people of color. No more paper products of any kind for racists. That may make some aspects of your life a little difficult but you'll find a way to deal with the problem.

Now you're thinking you'll use cloth. Think again. You can't use cotton; we got that from the Egyptians, the Chinese and the people in India. You can't use silk; we got that from the Chinese. You can't use linen; we got that from the Egyptians. You can't use any man-made fabrics because it takes electricity to make them. You can't use any woven fabrics because people of color were weaving fabrics while white folks were still looking for a 'rabbit skin to wrap their baby bunting in.'

I'll help you out here. Go out and dig up a rock. People of color didn't invent rocks. You can scratch your message on a rock. But don't use the alphabet to convey your thought; we got our alphabet from the Egyptians and the Phoenicians, still more people of color. You must draw pictures to convey your message.

If you intend to send any statistics in your letter you will, of course, express them in Roman numerals since the numeration system of choice in this country is Arabic. You may, however, use the alphabet and Arabic numerals to address your envelope, since I'm not sure that most US postal workers will be able to decipher zip codes expressed in your "from-whites-only" materials.

Once you get this rock wrapped and rolled and ready you may be tempted to run out and jump into your automobile to go down to the post office. Don't do it. Your car runs on rubber tires; we first got rubber from natives of South America who were people of color, so of course you'll give up all rubber products. Think of it: no more rubber for racists. That means we're going to have a lot more racists running around, eh?

Now you're deciding to ride your bicycle. Wrong again. The first successful bicycle frame in this country was developed by a black man.

No problem. You've decided to walk to the post office. Barefooted, I hope, unless you have hand sewn shoes, since the last that we use for sewing shoes together mechanically was first invented by a black man, Jan Ernst Matzileger.

Now when you get your shoes on and start your walk down to the post office, you may come to a stop light. Don't stop. The traffic signal was invented by a black male. You're going to go through that signal and when you do, some blue-eyed fool is going to come tearing down the street in his car, run that signal just like you did, hit you and knock you galley west. They're going to rush you to a hospital where they'll probably want to give you a blood transfusion using stored plasma. Don't take it. A Black man, Dr. Charles Drew, developed that process during the Second World War, so you'll never again take a blood transfusion using stored plasma.

Now all of this may be giving you a headache and you may

be tempted to take an aspirin. Resist the temptation, at all costs, for we got our first pain deadening chemicals from Native Americans who were and are people of color. You'll learn to live with the pain.

Perhaps you're one of those people who eat to relieve his/her tension and you're ready to race to the refrigerator for relief. Well, be very careful what you choose to munch on, because over 50% of the foods found in the average kitchen came to us from people color. Perhaps you enjoy a peanut butter and jelly sandwich. You can't use peanut butter; it was developed with the input of a black man, George Washington Carver, at Iowa State University in Ames, Iowa. You can't use bread because people of color were eating bread before white people knew they were hungry. However, white people may have been instrumental in making jam and jelly because everybody knows that white folks love sugar. So here's what you do. Slap a gob of jelly on your hand and lick it off. That can be the racist's PB&J sandwich.

Now you may be tempted to buttress your belief in white superiority by quoting from the Bible. Please be aware that the basic tenets of every major religion on the face of the earth originated in societies of people of color.

As you can see, a committed racist, and I think they all should be committed, who lives his/her belief in white superiority, may not live very comfortably or very long, but at least they'll die happy. But, about those funeral customs…

13. Racism is not something "out there." It is not found only in a large city or in the south or where people of color live. Racism is within each of us. It has been planted there by a racist society and is being nurtured by those with whom we communicate. People from little all-white communities in the Midwest who have never been in the company of people of color carry the

stereotypes of those who are different that their community has created for them. The presence of those stereotypes is obvious in the language they use and the behaviors they exhibit when they encounter people of color, or when they read about, hear about, think about, or talk about those whom they have been conditioned to think of as non-white.

14. The Pope said in February of 1989 that you can't be a Christian and a racist; the two are mutually exclusive. Therefore, those of you who choose to maintain your Christianity will have to give up your racism. And those who choose to maintain their racism will have to give up their Christianity. I know people who will give up their Christianity rather than their racism because they have seen proof in this country that racism is stronger than Christianity. If it isn't, why is the racism in this "Christian Nation" increasing drastically even as you read this? I'm relieved that the Pope finally spoke out. Now if we can just get him to address sexism....

15. "Good deeds will not go long unpunished." If, as a result of reading this book, you become even more determined to actively work at reducing the racism, sexism, ageism, homophobia and ethnocentrism in this society, be prepared to "suffer the slings and arrows" of outraged others. You'll soon need a support group, so I'd suggest that you share this material with someone you trust, and then organize a 12-step program for Recovering Racists. You think I'm being facetious? Think again. Habits of a lifetime are hard to break, particularly when the society responds positively to perpetuation of those habits and negatively to attempted change. Remember this: Some people grow older while others grow up. It's a choice you make. It's time for us to stop raising children and start raising adults.

26 What To Do...

Okay, so how do we start these changes? Give us some help, you say. Here are a few suggestions that you might try. Now, don't try to do them all at once. Choose one and do it for a month. Record the results and then choose another.

1) Examine your own racist attitudes, beliefs and behavior. How many of the following statements have you made or heard and refused to confront?

My great grandparents had to struggle to make it in this country. Why is it so different for blacks? If your grandparents were white the chances are pretty good they chose to come to this country. The majority of the blacks living in this country today had great grandparents who had no choice in the matter. Furthermore, the great grandparents of the blacks had to struggle at least as hard as your forbearers did. But all that is irrelevant, in fact. The question is, why should blacks have to work like your great grandparents did, while you are able to relax? I never owned slaves, so why should I have to pay for what happened in the past? You aren't being held responsible for the past; you're being expected to act responsibly in the present in order to construct a better future for us all.

I can't be held responsible for the activities of racist institutions. Of course you can! You, as an individual, have the power to affect change. You know it. Stop the denial and just do it.

You can't legislate morality.

Nonsense. We do it all the time. If everyone believed that, we'd still have slavery and women wouldn't be able to vote.

(Said to a black man) When I see you I don't see you black.

Why not? Is there something disgraceful or distasteful about black skin? Do you see the person green or orange? Are you unable to relate to a black person and so you must deny the blackness? Do you see gender? Height? Age?

Educated, mature, religious people don't exhibit racist behaviors.

Who writes the textbooks and pass the laws and run the lending institutions and police departments and schools, only the uneducated, immature and non-religious people?

Blacks just need to get educated and use that and the ballot to get their rights.

Who dictates what constitutes education in this country and who chooses those for whom we will be allowed to vote? This is a denial of the power of institutionalized racism.

When I see people I don't see people as black or brown or yellow or red. I just see people as people.

Why is 'white' never included in that list? This is an attempt to deny people the right to be different. Do you see people as old, young, male, female, etc, etc?

I've been this way all my life and I'm too old to change now.

No, you aren't. If your job, your income, your marriage, your family or your life depended on your behaving in a non-racist manner, you could do it. SO DO IT!

Only the dead are incapable of behavioral and attitudinal change.

2) Openly confront the next racist, sexist, ageist, homophobic joke or remark made in your presence. And don't apologize for making the offender uncomfortable. You aren't violating their freedom of speech; you are exercising your own. Only when those of us who are opposed to racism are as willing to speak out as the racists are will we begin to eradicate racism. It's working with smoking, isn't it?

3) Become aware of the racism in slogans, advertising, TV programs, news broadcasts and textbooks. Point them out and discuss them with your kids.

4) Form a study group to read and discuss the items on the bibliography at the end of this book. You must educate yourself where racism is concerned. The educational establishment in this country is for the purpose of schooling people. You take the schooling you got in the institution and use it to get educated.

5) Subscribe to a publication published by and for a culture other than your own. Leave it out in plain sight where your friends and associates might see it and question your interest in it.

6) Get a copy of the Peters Projection map of the world from your local map store, have it laminated, and present it to your child's teacher for use in the classroom. Do this with every class s/he enters. By the time your child gets through school, every grade level will have been exposed to that map. Be sure you point out the differences between it and the Mercator Projection, which is probably the one they're presently using.

7) Investigate your school's textbooks, visual aids, programs and policies in terms of their treatment of the issues of racism, sexism, ageism, homophobia, and ethnocentrism. Suggest changes where they are needed. Volunteer to help them to solve some of the problems.

8) Support non-racist companies with your dollar power.

9) Contribute time, money, and energy to agencies, programs, and organizations that actively confront the problems of the '-isms'.

10) Learn a language other than your own and use it!
11) Turn off you TV and pick up a book and read it! My first suggestion would be <u>The Giver</u>, by Lois Lowry, or <u>Faces at the Bottom of the Well</u> by Derek Bell or <u>Rage of a Privileged Class</u> by Ellis Cose, <u>The Myth Of Race</u>, by Robert Wald Sussman, <u>The Birth Dearth</u>, by Ben Wattenberg. The Sussman book, is a fair, intelligent, well-researched, and informative definition of where we are and how we got here, where the topic of 'race' is concerned. The Wattenberg book is a disturbing, racist rant against those people of different colors, who, according to the author, are trying to take over this white man's land, and what we must do to prevent that from happening.
12) BOYCOTT BIGOTRY!!! WITH GUSTO!!!

MOMENTS TO REMEMBER:

The following are some isolated incidents that I remember with, in some cases, awful clarity and, in other cases with great joy.

The young grad assistant in a college in Illinois who, as he drove me to the airport the morning after my lecture said,

"Well, Ms. Elliott, I agree with most of what you said, but you've made my job more difficult".

"Why is that?" I asked, in total ignorance.

"Well, I won't be able to work with these people in the same way, now," he replied.   "Why is that" I wondered.

"Because you've taken away their ignorance." OH MY GOD! Did he not realize who the ignorant one was? Did he not know that the Black students had been practicing tolerance in order to get along with HIM? What did I do? Did I chastise and berate him for his insensitivity? HELL, NO! I did what blacks do. I practiced tolerating him because I needed something from him and I couldn't afford to offend him at that point.

The white woman who, in a workshop at a major corporation said, "I don't dislike blacks: when I see one, I just say to myself, 'There but for the Grace of God go I'". THINK about that! She is actually convinced that God loved her so much that He made her white! We had a short but meaningful discussion of the situation, at that point.

The young black male accompanying us to the airport after a college lecture who said that he knew he had to suffer, and was willing to, because the Bible said he must. When I said,
"Where in the Bible did you read that?"

He said, "The Bible says, 'Suffer the little children to come unto me,' doesn't it?" I was shocked to think that some well-meaning religious leader or Sunday-school teacher had allowed (encouraged?) him to think that the suffering that he experiences because of the ignorance of this society was ordained by God. I explained to him that, in that context, to suffer means to allow or permit or, perhaps, tolerate, but it doesn't mean the little children have to suffer, in order to be in the presence of God. He was relieved to tears, and I was madder than a wet hen, to think that he'd spent his life, up to that point, accepting pain in the name of religion.

In the UK film How Racist Are You? the white teacher who describes her surprise at seeing that the little black girl who has gotten a cut on her arm while on the playground, "is pink under the skin, just like the rest of us."

There are, as you've noticed, several places in this material, where I've repeated ideas that I think are extremely important. These ideas aren't original with me; I've learned them from people who have been on the receiving end of the power and ignorance of racism all their lives.

There will be those who will say, "What about the racism that happens when blacks discriminate against whites? Isn't that just as bad as racism from whites against blacks?" Angry behavior by people without power is a reaction to the stereotyping that has been part of our conditioning for about 400 years. If you want to stop that angry reaction, stop abusing people on the basis of your ignorance about skin color and the human race. Skin color isn't the problem; ignorance is.

There will also be those who will claim that Affirmative Action is discriminatory behavior intended to advance blacks, at the expense of white males. Think that one over very carefully, in view of the fact that the most numerous beneficiaries of Affirmative Action policies are white females. Furthermore, instead of calling these programs 'Affirmative Action,' we might better label them, "Delayed Justice," since the Constitution of the United States guarantees every American citizen 'equitable treatment under the law.'

Before you sit down to compose an angry letter expressing your displeasure and disagreement with some of the things you've read here, I suggest that you read the following material which is the forward to William Peters' book, <u>A Class Divided, Then and Now</u>. It was written by Kenneth Clark, who was the originator of the black and white doll studies. It says:

"A major and inescapable goal of institutions is to broaden the perspective of human beings – to develop a truly functional empathy – to free human beings from the constrictions of ignorance, superstition, hostility, and other forms of inhumanity. Jane Elliott's contribution… demonstrates that it is possible to educate and produce a class of human being united by understanding, acceptance, and empathy."

As a final warning, may I suggest that the next time you hear someone say that slavery, the Civil War, and segregation are all things of the past, you visit a prison, you talk to some of the southern gentlemen who had determined that no black man would ever be President of the US, and you visit practically any small town in the Midwest, or any big city, anywhere in the US. Remind those that say that segregation is a thing of the past, that there are more children in the United States attending segregated schools today than there were previous to Brown vs. Board of Education in 1954.

Racism is alive and well in the U.S. of A.

To purchase documentaries about the BE/BE Exercise and a list of additional suggested readings, please go to my website: **www.janeelliott.com**

Conclusion

In the years since I started to write this book, my family has gone through marriages and divorces, births and deaths, illness and health, horrendous sorrow and unbelievable joy, and still we encounter the hatred of those who believe in the idea of the superiority of the white race; and the gratitude of those who realize and understand that there is no white race, who understand that there is only one race, the Human Race, which evolved in sub-Saharan Africa from 140,00 to 280,000 years ago, and that we are all descendants of those first black people. It has only been about 500 years that people have been led to believe in the myth of race. I hope that it doesn't take another 500 years for us to stop believing in this idiocy, and to wake up to appreciate all the color groups, and to delete from our vocabulary, the word 'race', when referring to groups of people of different colors.

Epilogue

To quote Carrie, a participant in the BE/BE Exercise filmed at Bard College,

"If you didn't learn anything from what happened here, today, it sucks to be you.

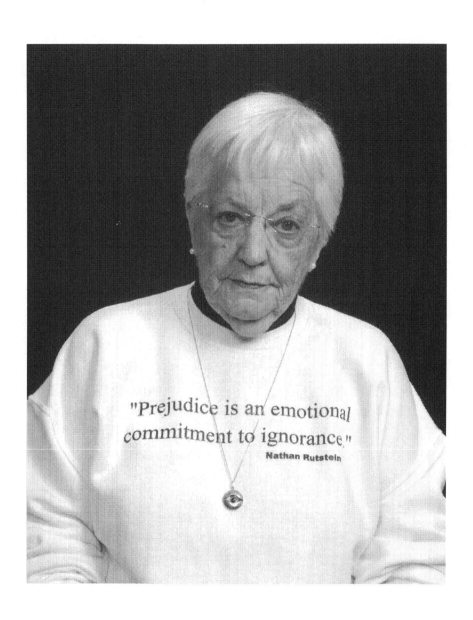

ABOUT THE AUTHOR

Jane Elliott is an educator who began her career in a third-grade classroom in Riceville, Iowa, and over the past 50 years has become an educator of people of all ages all over the US and abroad. The Blue-eyed, Brown-eyed Exercise, which she used to help her students to understand Martin Luther King, Jr.'s work, has been cited and studied by psychologists and sociologists all over the world. Elliott lives in a remodeled schoolhouse 21 miles from where she was born.

She is steadfast in her belief that there is only one race on the face of the earth, THE HUMAN RACE, and we are all members of that race.

Bibliography

AGEISM
- Comfort, Alex. A Good Age. London: Mitchell Beazley Publishers, 1976
- Spark, Muriel. Memento Mori. New York: Putnam, 1982

ANTI-SEMITISM
- Fension, Fanye. Playing For Time. New York: Berkeley, 1983.
- Leitner, Isabella. Fragments of Isabella: A Memoir of Auschwitz. New York: Dell, 1978
- Seigel, Aranka. Upon the Head od the Goat. New York: Farrar, Straus, and Giroux, 1983.
- Weisel, Elie. A Jew Today. New York: Random House, 1978
- Weisel, Elie. Night. New York: Bantam, 1982.
- Yaseen, Leonard C. The Jesus Connection. New York: Crossroads, 1985.
- Zyskind, Sara. Stoeln Years. Minneapolis: Lerner, 1981.

HOMOPHOBIA
- Jennings, Kevin. One Teacher in 10. Los Angeles, CA: Alycon Publications, Inc., 1994
- Pharr, Suzanne. Homophobia: A Weapon of Sexism. Inverness, CA: Chardon Press, 1988.

RACISM
- Alexander, Michelle. The New Jim Crow. New York: The New Press, 2010.
- Aliport, Gordon. The Nature of Prejudice. Cambridge, Massachusetts: Addison Wesley, 1976.
- Burton, M. Garlinda. Never Say Nigger Again. Nashville, TN 37205: James C. Winston, 1976
- Chu, Louis. Eat a Bowl of Tea. New Jersey: Lyle Stuart, Inc., 1961.
- Clark, Kenneth. Prejudice and Your Child. Middleton, CT:

Wesleyan, 1986.

- Cobbe, Price, and Crier, William. Black Rage. New York: Basic Books, 1960.
- Cone, James H. Martin and Malcolm and America. Maryknoll, NY: Orbis Books, 1991.
- Cose, Ellis. The Rage of a Privileged Class. New York, NY: Harper Collins, 1993.
- Deloria, Vine. Custer Died For Your Sins. New York: Avon, 1970.
- Deloria, Vine. God is Red. New York: Dell, 1983.
- Deloria, Vine. We Talk, You Listen. New ork, MacMillan, 1970.
- Friedman, Thomas L. From Beirut to Jerusalem. New York: Doubleday, 1989.
- Hecker, Andrew. Two Nations: Black and White. Separate, Hostile, and Unequal. MacMillan (H.B.) Ballantine (P.B.), 1992.
- Homokawa, Bill. The Quiet Americans. New York: Morrow, 1972.
- Houston, Jeane and James D. Farewell to Manzanar. New York, 1974.
- Kane, Pearl Rock and Orsini, Alfonso, J. The Color of Excellence. New York, NY: TeachersCollege Press, Columbia University, 2003.
- Kennedy, Randall. Nigger. New York, NY: Pantheon Books, 2002.
- Kochman, Thomas. Black and White Styles in Conflict. Chicago: University of Chicago Press, 1981.
- Landsman, Julie. A White Teacher Talks About Race. Lanham, MD: Scarecrow Press Inc., 2001.
- Lincoln, C. Eric. Race, Religions and the Continuing American Dilemma. New York, NY: Hill and Wang, 1999.
- Mathabane, Mark. Kaffir Boy. New York: MacMillan, 1986.
- Mirande, Alfredo. The Chicago Experiment: An Alternative Perspective. Notre Dame, 1985.
- Morrison, Toni. The Bluest Eye. New York: Washington

Square, 1972.

- Nam, Vicki. <u>Yell-Oh Girls</u>. New York, NY: Harper Collins, 2001.
- Peters, William. <u>A Class Divided; Then and Now</u>. New Haven, CT: Yale, 1987.
- Rodriguez, Richard. <u>Hunger of Memory: The Education of Richard Rodriguez</u>. New York: Bantom, 1982.
- Rutstein, Nathan. <u>The Racial Conditioning of Our Children</u>. Albion, MI: The National Resource Center for the Healing of Racism, 2001.
- Ryan, William. <u>Blaming the Victim</u>. New York: Random House, 1972.
- Shipler, David K. <u>Arab and Jew</u>. New York: Penguin Books, 1986.
- Siberman, Charles. <u>Crisis is Black and White</u>. New York: Random House, 1972.
- Smith, Lillian. <u>Killers of the Dream</u>. New York: Norton, 1978.
- Stiglitz, Joseph E. <u>The Price of Inequality</u>. New York: Norton, 2012.
- Tan, Amy. <u>The Kitchen God's Wife</u>. G.P. Putnam's Sons, 1991.
- Urrea, Luis Alberto. <u>Across the Wire: Life and Hard Times on the Mexican Border</u>. New York: Anchor Books, 1993.
- Urrea, Luis Alberto. <u>The Devil's Highway</u>. New York, NY: Little, Brown, And Co., 2004.
- Walker, Alice. <u>The Color Purple</u>. New York: Washington Square, 1982.
- Walsh, Joan. <u>What's the Matter with White People</u>. New Jersey: John Wiley & Sons, 2012.
- Wattenberg, Ben. <u>The Birth Dearth</u>. New York: Pharos, 1987.
- Weatherford, Jack. <u>Native Roots</u>. New York, NY: Ballantine Books, 1991.
- White, Joseph L. <u>The Psychology of Blacks</u>. Englewood, Cliffs, NJ: Prentice Hall, Inc., 1984.
- Williams, Juan. <u>Eyes on the Prize</u>. New York: Viking,

1987.
- Wright, Richard. <u>Black Boy</u>. New York: Harper and Row, 1969.
- Yette, Samuel F. <u>Choice: The Issue of Black Survival in America</u>. Springs, MD: Cottage Books, 1982.

SEXISM
- Atwood, Margaret. <u>The Handmaid's Tale</u>. New York: Ballantine, 1985.
- Eisler, Raine. <u>The Chalice and the Blade</u>. New York: Harper and Row, 1987.
- Gilligan, Carol. <u>Is A Different Voice</u>. Cambridge, MA: Harvard University Press, 1982.
- Smith, Lillian. <u>Killers of the Dream</u>. New York: Norton, 1978.
- Wilson-Schaef, Anne. <u>Women's Reality</u>. San Francisco: Harper and Row, 1985.
- Wolf, Naomi. <u>The Beauty Myth</u>. Toronto: Random House, 1990.

GENERAL
- Carter, Forrest. <u>The Education of Little Tree</u>. Albuquerque, NM: 1986.
- Clavell, James. <u>The Children's Story</u>. New York: Delacorte, 1981.
- Friedman, Thomas. <u>The World is Flat</u>. New York, NY: Farrar, Straus, and Giroux, 2005.
- Glassner, Barry. <u>The Culture of Fear</u>. New York, NY: Basic Book, 1999.
- Golden, Harry. <u>Only in America</u>. Cleveland, World, 1959.
- Golden, Harry. <u>For 2 Cent Plain</u>. Cleveland: World, 1959.
- Golden, Harry. <u>Enjoy! Enjoy!</u>. Cleveland: World, 1960.
- Lakoff, George. <u>Don't Think of an Elephant</u>. White River Junction, VT: Chelsea Green Pub Co., 2004.
- Loewen, James W. <u>Lies My Teacher Told Me</u>. New York, NY: The New Press, 1995.
- Pauling, Chris. <u>Introducing Buddhism</u>. New York, NY:

Barnes and Noble Books, 1990.

- Ruiz, Don Miguel. <u>The Four Agreements</u>. San Rafael, CA: Amber-Allen Publishing, 1997.
- Simons, Abramms, Hopkins, and Johnson. <u>Cultural Diveristy</u>. Princeton, NJ: Peterson's/Pacesetter Books, 1996.
- Stern-LaRosa, and Bettman, Ellen H. <u>Hate Hurts</u>. New York, NY: Scholastic, Inc., 2000.
- Zinn, Howard. <u>A People's History of the United States</u>. New York: Harper Collins Publishers, 1990.

63088336R00140

Made in the USA
Charleston, SC
27 October 2016